TUSCANY

Jonathan Keates

TUSCANY

Photography by Charlie Waite

GEORGE
PHILIP

British Library Cataloguing in Publication Data
Keates, Jonathan, *1946–*
Tuscany.
1. Italy. Tuscany. Visitors' guides
I. Title
914.5'504928
ISBN 0-540-01176-2

Text © Jonathan Keates 1988
Photographs © Charlie Waite 1988
Maps © George Philip 1988

First published by George Philip,
59/60 Grosvenor Street, London W1X 9DA

Printed in Italy

Half-title illustration **The Virgin and Child with St John by Luca della Robbia, at Montepulciano.**

Title-page illustration
Barga's romanesque cathedral has the Apuan Alps as a dramatic backdrop.

Contents

To Lisa

FECIT HOC OP GRUA MONSMAG ✠ BON: ET ADODAT FRATER EIVS

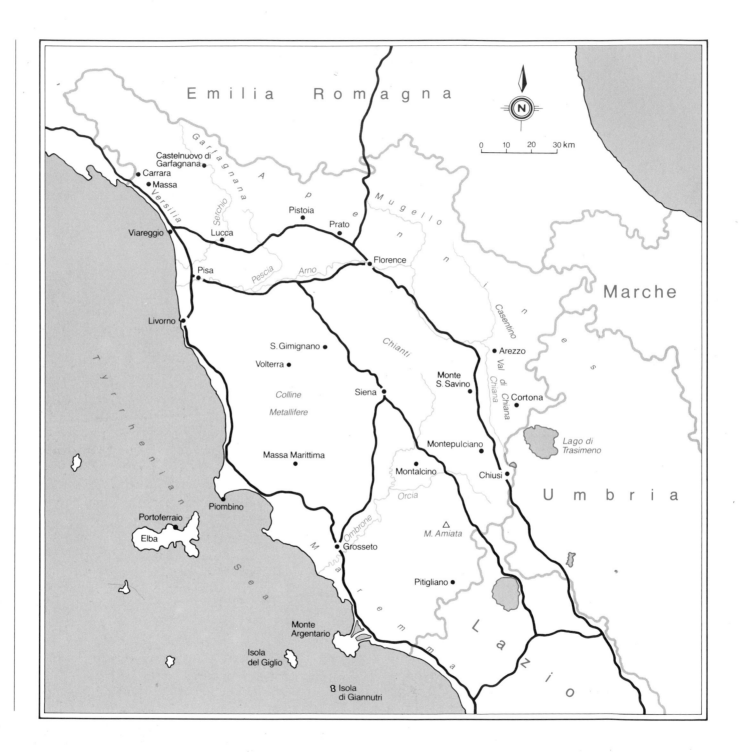

Introduction

There is something truly awful about Tuscany. Its landscape is overwhelmingly beautiful, its cities, some of the most perfect statements of the urban principle ever formulated, are prodigally endowed with the greatest works of art, its people are welcoming and the food and drink which greet the traveller are some of the best in the world.

For such reasons I am no sooner there than I long to escape. The sheer superabundance is difficult to bear and the interminable paeans of praise to Tuscany on the lips of everyone since the fall of the Roman empire become intolerable, driving me across the Apennines to Bologna, up to Milan, down to Rome, over to Venice, anywhere rather than stay amid this devastating perfection.

It makes Tuscans themselves decidedly smug. There are moments when, attempting to itemize Italy's boundless gifts to the Western world in purely human terms, you start to wonder who was *not* Tuscan. Michelangelo, Leonardo, Giotto, Cellini, Dante, Boccaccio, Petrarch, Machiavelli, Galileo and Puccini are merely the best-known names, and practically every small town has its square, its statue and its marble plaque on the humble birthplace to commemorate the country boy who set off to Florence or Siena to be a professional genius. True Tuscans every one, they loved their native earth best of all, and the beauty of much of their art lies in its loyal reflections of home ground. This is, after all, the region in which the standard form of contemporary Italian speech evolved, though to hear native Tuscans talking, with their syncopated vowels, their substitutions of soft and hard sounds and the notorious aspirated 'h', which turns a phrase such as *quanto costa questo?* (how much does this cost?) into *huanto hosta huesto?*, you would hardly appreciate this claim to linguistic primacy.

For a civilization so intensely urban as Italy's has always been, the region's history features few significant disturbances of the traditional agricultural landscape. It is still possible to walk into the background, as it were, of a Fra Angelico panel, a Giotto fresco or a Sienese *quattrocento* altarpiece, yet each of these will mirror the extraordinary diversity of landscape within Tuscany itself. The inhabitants have no illusions about this countryside. It is there to be planted, farmed and exploited, and only the fact that much of the terrain is so hilly and rugged has rescued it from the kind of visual tedium to be found in the intensively cultivated plains of Lombardy and Emilia away to the north.

Each area of Tuscany has its individual name, firmly linked to a precise local identity. The Garfagnana is a stretch of deep valleys and mountain spurs in the north-western corner of the region, a territory whose thin coastal strip is known as the Versilia. To the south, beyond Pisa, begins the broad, undulating country of the Maremma, stretching down to Grosseto and the southern border with Lazio in a series of bald hills, plateaux, pine woods and scrubby heathlands. The eastern edge of the Maremma is bounded by the Val d'Orcia and the Val di Chiana, river valleys dominated by the three towns of Arezzo, Cortona and Montepulciano. At the heart of the province lies Siena, with the bare chalky uplands of the *crete senesi* to the south and the great crest of Monte Amiata beyond. Northwards, the Chianti district spreads in a prospect of vineyards and wooded hills almost to the gates of Florence itself, at whose back are the wild ridges of the Mugello and the Casentino. West of Florence, the fertile plain of the Arno becomes the market garden of Tuscany, reaching to Lucca and its green Lucchesia, whence the best olive oil traditionally derives.

Within such settings the profile of a town or village preserves certain unchanging features relating it to the political and social history of the region. In this context some Italian words are more resonant than their English equivalents, such as the *borgo*, an ancient fortified settlement, with its *rocca*, fortress, *duomo*, cathedral and *parrochiale* or *pieve*, parish church, centres of authority for the surrounding *contado*, the territory ruled by a town. After a little travelling in Tuscany you can easily start to read its cities as individual chronicles, unravelling the past experience of each from the evidence of building styles, coats of arms, badges, frescoes and inscriptions.

It would be wrong, however, to think of Tuscany's past as something cohesive in quite the same way as that of England or America. As a political entity, which it was until 1860, it grew by very slow additions, its last portion of territory being acquired as late as 1847. The very word *Toscana* seems to have evolved, via the early medieval *Tuscia*, from a variant on the name of its first notable inhabitants, the people called the Etruscans.

At its widest, Etruria spread over the Apennines to include Bologna, and south along the coast beyond Rome. Writers on Italy often refer to the Etruscans as 'mysterious' – a convenient adjective if you have nothing to say about them. Actually, we know a great deal regarding Etruscan life, religion and art, and some, if not all, of their language has been deciphered. The best book about them, George Dennis's *Cities and Cemeteries of Etruria*, is also one of the most engaging narratives of Italian travel: it was written nearly 150 years ago and urgently needs reprinting.

Though the Romans ultimately crushed the Etruscans, they considered it very grand to be able to boast Etruscan descent, and Maecenas, the great Augustan patron of Horace and Virgil, was immensely proud of the fact that his family came from the old Etruscan capital, Arezzo, whose archaeological museum is named after him. Little of Roman Tuscany remains – the amphitheatre at Lucca, the theatre at Volterra and not much else except the ground plans of cities and legends of their foundation, a scatter of sarcophagi and scores of columns re-utilized in romanesque churches.

It was the Longobards, Teutonic invaders in the sixth century AD, who stamped their presence most forcefully on northern Italy, not merely in hundreds of place names and words of Germanic origin, but in the entire organization of society. Until the early twelfth century, 'Tuscia' was a marquisate of the Holy Roman

---

Terraced fields and olive groves make up the landscape of central Tuscany, seen here around San Miniato.

This eighteenth-century stucco medallion adorns a palace at Bagni di Lucca.

Empire, administered by feudal landlords in the name of the imperial vicars. The last of these, a woman so remarkable that her name is blessed in Tuscany to this day, was the Countess Matilda (1045–1115), 'intrepid in her warlike valour as much as in her faith', the friend of popes and saints, the terror of kings, admired and courted by everybody from the Byzantine Emperor to the sons of William the Conqueror, a Tuscan girl born at San Miniato.

At her death the Pope laid claim not merely to the estates she had actually left him, but to those she held from the Emperor. The resulting struggle endured for almost two centuries, dividing the cities of Tuscany and growing more bitter at the death of the powerful Emperor Frederick II in 1250. Each of the two parties was known by a name associated with the imperial claimant it supported, Welf and Waiblingen, italianized to *Guelfo* and *Ghibellino*. The Guelphs backed the Pope, the Ghibellines championed imperial autonomy, and their running feuds, often setting one area of a city against the other, made an indelible mark on the culture of the Italian Middle Ages.

Against this stormy background, a single figure stands out more boldly than all the others, a man whose profoundly personal, often maddeningly idiosyncratic response to the events of his time has clothed the dry bones of historical fact with an imperishable allure. Dante Alighieri was born in Florence in 1265, into a family of decayed gentlefolk, and early on became involved in furious contests within the city itself, turning on that contentious issue of whether or not to compromise with foreign invaders which has remained a constant in Italian history. Misery and frustration marked both his public and private life: in 1302 he was sentenced *in absentia* to burning alive, and spent his remaining 19 years in exile, dying at Ravenna in 1321. He never satisfied his longing for Beatrice Portinari, the girl he met when she was eight and he was nine, and the news of her premature death in 1290 shattered him so much that he transformed her into his immortal muse, invoked in all his major works.

The poem he completed during his wanderings, *La Divina Commedia*, is the record of a mystical journey through the three realms of Hell, Purgatory and Paradise. Its assertion of the authority of Tuscan as a literary language was part of a broader appeal to a sense of unity among Italians, an aspect of the work which reinforced its classic status in later centuries. As sustained literary expression it is unequalled save by Homer and Shakespeare, and many foreigners have learnt Dante's native tongue solely in order to read him.

The stillness of afternoon in the streets of San Gimignano.

The poem's unique quality is the way in which Dante uses significant people and events of medieval Tuscany as his raw material. He seems to have known about everything and everyone who mattered, and flings them with unsparing candour into his piquant brew. We remember figures such as Pia de' Tolomei, Count Ugolino and Brunetto Latini because of what Dante says about them or makes them say, and the places where they flourished and died impress us the more vividly because of the way in which the memory of his words has coloured them like the veins in a piece of marble.

Dante's Florence was already a city of tremendous mercantile wealth, whose noble families were the bankers of Europe, and the fourteenth century saw its gradual acquisition of most of northern and eastern Tuscany. The assumption of power by the Medici family in 1434 consolidated the Florentine achievement, that of a city state whose major role on the European political stage was enhanced by the intensity of her artistic culture, a profusion of excellence unsurpassed before or since.

This concentration of genius within a single city, during a period of little more than fifty years, is something astonishing. As the shiploads of 'brown Greek manuscripts' arrived in the ports of Italy, and the art, literature and ethics of the classical world were enthusiastically rediscovered, Florence became a worthy rival of Periclean Athens or Augustan Rome. Brunelleschi and Michelozzo sounded new harmonies of architectural proportion and design, Masaccio and Botticelli brought an undreamt-of substance and strength to the representation of man in his natural dimension, echoed by the originality of sculptors such as Donatello, Ghiberti, Benedetto da Maiano and Mino da Fiesole. The first Florentine printing-press was set up in 1471, the earliest public library in Italy was opened in the convent of San Marco and Marsilio Ficino, son of Cosimo de' Medici's doctor, presided over a Platonic academy, which met in the gardens of villas and monasteries to interpret and discuss the Greek philosopher's ideals.

The Medici and their supporters were no better or worse than most other contemporary tyrants and their followers: we remember Cosimo and Lorenzo, however, not for their cruelty or ruthlessness, but as lovers of poetry and music, patrons of sculpture, painting and architecture and friends to scholarship. Florentine capitalism was as avaricious and self-seeking as our own, but the merchants of the Renaissance, for all their obsession with market forces, continued to value and promote art and learning as integral components of the common good, wisely realizing that in the end Florence would survive through the enduring achievements of the human spirit rather than by the cash flow and enterprise culture which sustained them.

Shaken and occasionally toppled as the Medici were, by French invasion, by the Dominican zealot Girolamo Savonarola, by revivals of the city's ancient republicanism, they clung on, and it was a distant cousin of Lorenzo whose seizure of power in 1537 sealed their dominion over Tuscany. Confirmed as Grand Duke in 1569, Cosimo I was determined to make his state the most powerful and economically efficient in Italy. His family coat of arms, six scarlet balls on a yellow ground, is everywhere, as is his image, rivalled only by that of Queen Victoria in its plethora of representations. The Medici Grand Dukes, morose, eccentric and supernaturally ugly (Charles II of England, whose mother was Cosimo I's great-granddaughter, was pure Medici in looks) nevertheless loved Tuscany and ruled it wisely and benevolently.

When the last of them, Gian Gastone, who had spent much of his later life in bed, died childless in 1737, his

---

A modern mosaic crowns the doorway of a church at Montepulciano.

realm passed to the Austrian Hapsburgs of the house of Lorraine, whose government of the duchy, at least until the Napoleonic Wars, was a model of rational enlightenment. This was the beginning of Florence's role as a haven of expatriates, led by a sizeable English colony which grew even more dominant after 1815. It was an intensely insular community, with its own chemist, grocer, Anglican church and cemetery, and the spectre of its separateness, enhanced by the arrival of the Americans during the nineteenth century, haunts Florentine life to this day. It was certainly not without its charm and romance, and the contribution made by Anglo-American scholarship to Italy's appreciation of her artistic patrimony is undeniably significant, but a consistent reluctance to mingle with Italians, allied to a sense of 'the natives' merely as quaintly roguish hotel porters, chambermaids, gallery attendants, cab-drivers and cooks, is an attitude which persists all too robustly.

As the most liberal and forward-looking state of early nineteenth-century Italy, Tuscany watched keenly while the rest of the peninsula chafed under Austria's bullying influence, and the Risorgimento, as the various movements for national independence are collectively labelled, grew to a head. The cardinal error of Grand Duke Leopold II in 1848 was both to underestimate the continuing strength of liberal sentiment and to betray the trust of the mass of his subjects, who had genuinely appreciated his bumbling but benign rule, by beefing up the Austrian military presence in Florence and starting to govern with untypical severity. When he finally went into exile in 1860 and the Grand Duchy became part of the new kingdom of Italy, it was significantly observed that Tuscany, efficiently and progressively administered, was unlikely to gain much by the change. *The Effects of Good Government* is the subject of a famous medieval fresco by the Sienese painter Ambrogio Lorenzetti. It is also the fortunate legacy which has given this region so much of the beauty and confidence it continues to assert to the world.

At the centre of it all is Florence, a city which has never forgotten its role either as the ultimate urban paradigm of renaissance civilization or as the capital, from 1865 to 1871, of Italy itself, yet a place which can never wholly shake off its provincialism. It is not nowadays the capital of anything very much, and I have always found something slightly cold and unwelcoming about it, a certain hostile detachment in the hard cubes of its palaces and a notable absence of the sort of visceral popular culture produced by Naples, Venice or Rome. In its passive acceptance of the world's homage for the sheer impacted mass of wonderful things crowded within it, the city always reminds me of Ingres's famous portrait of Madame Moitessier, a superbly upholstered sophisticate turning a mask of inert perfection to the onlooker.

And yet . . . and yet. . . . Who has not been awed and enraptured by this beauty? I think of a certain hillside at Terzano, to the south of the city, where my heart always misses a beat or two when, turning the bend in the road, I catch a first glimpse of 'the most beautiful of cities, with the golden Arno shot through the breast of her like an arrow' as Elizabeth Barrett Browning ecstatically wrote, with Brunelleschi's dome and Giotto's tower offering their abiding reassurances. I think of a view from a window in the evening, when, within a frame of olive and cypress, the river glows like molten metal and the palaces and towers turn black against the livid sunset.

Where Florence eclipses every other city is in its extraordinary fusion of the urban and the rustic. Standing in the Piazza del Duomo with the clatter and fume of buses and tourists around you, or threading your way through the narrow lanes between Palazzo

The simple beauty of medieval San Gimignano.

Vecchio and Santa Croce, with a ribbon of pavement like a tightrope and daredevil motorscooter jockeys ready to buzz you as soon as you step off it, you would be foolish to ignore what the place is trying to tell you in terms of the inalienable superiority of town life. Yet cross the river, walk up through the courtyard of Palazzo Pitti, climb the steep terraces to the topmost level of the Boboli gardens and look over the wall: the journey from Piazza della Signoria will have taken you barely twenty minutes, yet beyond lies the pure Tuscan countryside of olive groves and orchards, with a scatter of villas over the surrounding hills.

It is the sense of definition established by these hills, with their umbrella pines and feathery, dark-leaved ilexes, which gives Florence the profile it has miraculously preserved. Anywhere else in Europe would by now have had freeways and flyovers driven across it. Florence may often be a misery for both motorist and pedestrian, but it hangs on fiercely to its visual identity and we are singularly fortunate in being able to see today more or less what was known and cherished by such diverse figures as D. H. Lawrence, Henry James and Queen Victoria, united in their love for the place.

The presence of a significant past is so powerful in Florence that I should like to take it for granted that certain of its buildings, paintings and sculptures will form an essential grammar of civilized reference for all visitors to the city. Alas, this is not always so. I recall a despairing morning with some newly-arrived acquaintances whose sole wish was to tour the smart shops of the streets around Piazza della Repubblica in search of chic additions to their wardrobe. Shopping in Italy is fun because Italians have no stupid inhibitions about buying, selling or display, and shopping is indeed one of Florence's major pleasures, but browsing in Valentino or Armani without ever having looked at Ghiberti or Michelangelo is, in my resolutely old-fashioned view, a reprehensible heresy.

Any traveller arriving in Florence will at least visit the *Duomo* and the Baptistery, will brace himself for the very long queues for admission to the Uffizi gallery and will join the throng which gazes, with expressions ranging from the lubricious to the frankly bemused, at Michelangelo's *David* in the Accademia. He will admire the Pazzi Chapel at Santa Croce, the fundamental text of Brunelleschi's architectural language, begun in 1443 but only completed after the master's death. May I hope that he will also go to San Lorenzo and see the work of Michelangelo turned architect, in the almost unnerving fluidity of the library staircase and the carefully engineered sombreness of the New Sacristy, that he will cross the river and enjoy the pictures in Palazzo Pitti, an unforgettable document in the history of taste, and that he may even find his way to the church of the Carmine. Here the newly restored frescoes by Masaccio (1401–28) in the Brancacci chapel have been the Alpha and Omega of painting ever since the days when Raphael diligently scrutinized 'those old things of Masaccio's'.

Since this is not a guidebook in the ordinary sense, and since Florence needs a whole volume to itself, I can only direct you towards my own selection of individual objects and places, a mere handful of the city's visual delights. This is a personal choice, and I can already hear my art-historical friends, their aesthetic priorities tightly corseted after years of checking their references for articles in *The Burlington Magazine* and *The Journal of the Warburg and Courtauld Institutes* reprovingly murmuring: 'Of course, if it were me, I should have chosen. . . .' But it is not them, and anyway, to use the Italian phrase whose

The classic prospect of Florence from Bellosguardo, a view unchanged in five hundred years.

The Entombment, a panel from Lorenzo Ghiberti's superb bronze doors to the Baptistery, Florence.

Brunelleschi's dome, winner of a competition in 1420 and completed in 1436, strikes the keynote in the skyline of Florence.

polite translation is 'Who cares?', '*Chi se ne frega?*'

Start in Piazza del Duomo, where everyone should look at the bronze doors of the Baptistery and appreciate the significant difference between the two pairs by Lorenzo Ghiberti (1378–1455) traditionally used to distinguish gothic from renaissance. On your right is the late nineteenth-century façade of the *Duomo*, about whose drearily vacant interior writers on Florence tend to be more flowery than sincere, dwelling on its unquestioned importance in the history of architecture as the largest church in western Europe before 1500. Outside it is far more absorbing to the eye, partly because of the beauty of some of the sculpture, especially that of Nanni di Banco's Porta della Mandorla, but above all for the dome created by Filippo Brunelleschi (1377–1446), which represents one of the great triumphs of imaginative possibility, since nobody at the time believed the work could actually be brought about.

To see how Brunelleschi translated his vision into reality go round the back of the cathedral, and on the eastern side of the square you will find the Museo dell'Opera del Duomo, one of my favourite Florentine museums. Here are the block-and-tackle apparatus, the carpenter's and mason's tools, the plans and models used in bringing the whole enterprise together. Anyone who seriously believes that artists are frivolous and unnecessary should be shown these objects and their result, an enduring demonstration of human capability at its noblest.

Now go up to the first floor, where two of the most vital achievements of renaissance sculpture await you.

The *Cantorie*, or organ lofts, were made for the *Duomo* by Luca della Robbia (1431) and Donatello (1433), but the noise that comes from them is the far from solemn sound of the carved reliefs of little children, youths and maidens making a joyful noise on pipes and drums, obeying the Psalmist's instructions to 'praise him upon the lute and harp, praise him upon the loud cymbals'. The figures on della Robbia's panels have a decorous solemnity in total contrast to the wildly excited whirling of Donatello's cherubs, tumbling over one another in chuckling ecstasies of delight.

Via dei Servi from the *Duomo* takes you into a quiet, workaday quarter of Florence full of shops selling useful things for the house. At the end lies one of the town's handsomest open spaces, Piazza Santissima Annunziata, or, as it is generally written, SS Annunziata. What looks like the perfect ensemble of gracefully arched loggias was not originally conceived as such. The Ospedale degli Innocenti, by Brunelleschi (1421), with its little swaddled babies in terracotta by Andrea della Robbia (1435–1525) reminding us that this is the world's oldest foundling hospital, faces the Loggia of the Servites, begun in 1516 as an obvious gesture of symmetry. The effect of a coherent design is completed by the portico of the church after which the piazza is named.

You will admire Giambologna's statue of Grand Duke Ferdinand I, made from captured Turkish cannon, in the middle of the square, and, if you can see them adequately under the nineteenth-century glass roof which makes the place look like the pump-room at a spa, the frescoes in the Chiostro dei Voti by Andrea del Sarto, Pontormo and others. Go into the church, whose stunning baroque decoration is by Giovanni Battista Foggini (1652–1725), though the original plan, with little tunnel-like arches connecting the side chapels and a tribune inspired by a Roman temple, is by Michelozzo (1396–1472). On the left-hand side of the tribune rails is what I find one of the more hauntingly memorable examples of renaissance sculpture, Francesco da San Gallo's recumbent effigy of Angiolo Marzi Medici, Bishop of Arezzo, who died in 1546. He lies on his side, one hand upraised, and an astonishing expression of restless, squint-eyed cunning in his features, mingled with a sense of perpetual agony, as if the sculptor knew he was a hardened old sinner and had doomed him to an unending torment of polished alabaster. Opposite him, in an identical pose, is Foggini's Donato dell'Antella, whose abundant self-satisfaction merely makes things worse for the bishop. The guide writers never discuss Francesco's masterpiece: has any of them, I wonder, ever looked at it properly?

SS Annunziata is a very popular church with the Florentines. Expectant mothers, brides-to-be and students anxious for good exam results are all to be found at prayer there, and in former times it used to be hung with wax effigies of both the dead and the living, suspended from the ceiling on ropes. Lorenzo de'Medici's likeness was by Andrea Verrocchio and was dressed in the clothes he wore on the fateful Sunday, 26 April 1478, when he escaped death at the hands of Jacopo de' Pazzi. Spurred on by the pope, Jacopo had tried to murder him while at Mass in the *Duomo*.

It was Lorenzo's grandfather Cosimo who helped to found the Dominican convent of San Marco in 1436, which, as Vasari tells us, was 'held to be the best conceived and most beautiful and commodious convent of any in Italy, thanks to the virtue and industry of Michelozzo', who rebuilt and enlarged earlier monastic buildings on the site. It is probably just as well that tourists do not swarm through its cells and cloisters in quite such droves as they do elsewhere in Florence, and even on a crowded summer morning something of the air of that fervent time when Savonarola expounded scripture to the brothers 'and for an hour or two one seemed verily to be in Paradise,

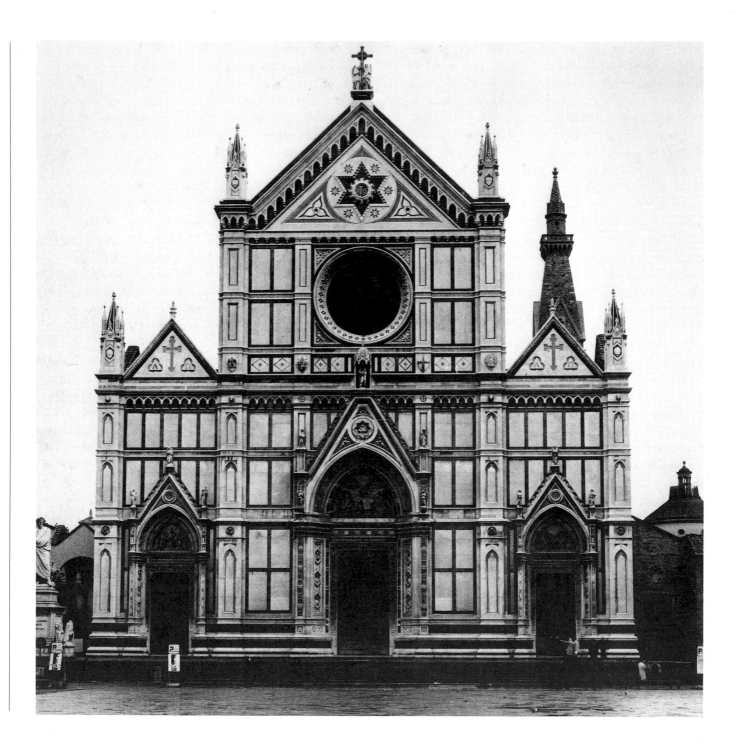

such charity and devotion and simplicity appeared in all' can still be found here. To reach San Marco, turn sharp right as you leave SS Annunziata, perhaps paying a visit to the Accademia on your way if you have not seen it already.

The presiding genius of San Marco is neither Cosimo il Vecchio nor Savonarola but the gentler, more companionable spirit of Fra Giovanni of Fiesole, 'il Beato Angelico' (1387–1455), whom you will meet again at Vicchio in the Mugello, where he was born. Nearly all his finest works are in the museum on the ground floor, and though Vasari's account of his life may be an admiring essay in hagiography, the painter's total assent to the validity of the miracles, signs, wonders and epiphanies which form the basis of Christian belief is something calculated to soften even the most cynical onlooker.

Fra Angelico's most impressive achievement as a fresco painter awaits you on the floor above, in the series of cells he decorated with various assistants between 1442 and 1447. Only nine of the wall paintings are definitely his, but his spirit breathes through the entire sequence (there are 44 in all) and the *Annunciation* at the head of the stairs, in which the Virgin seems intent on absorbing the unique truth of the Archangel's message, forms an ideal prelude. This was a scene he loved to paint, and as it is, for me, the most striking moment in any of the Gospels, I have no hesitation in sending you to look at his finest treatment of the episode, in the third cell on the left. The stark plainness of the scene is no mere act of monastic decorum, but an attempt to bring the perceived truth of this meeting of human and divine to life with only the simplest dimension of tangible reality to separate us from it.

Santa Croce's façade, paid for by an Englishman, Sir Francis Sloane, is a nineteenth-century addition to a medieval church.

Walk back towards Piazza del Duomo along Via Cavour and follow noisy Via dei Cerretani from the western side of the square. Striking down Via dei Banchi brings you out into the open space in front of Santa Maria Novella. This is the Dominican equivalent to the Franciscan Santa Croce. I have always found something too frigidly grand in the latter, the Pantheon of Italy's great men, whereas Santa Maria Novella, with its exhilarating marriage of Leon Battista Alberti's façade (1458–70) to the fourteenth-century gothic interior, has the sort of friendly unorthodoxy I love. Surely no one could fail to appreciate Masaccio's hermetically sombre *Trinity* and the bizarre frescoes by Filippino Lippi (1456–1504) on the east side of the choir, or to enjoy the unmistakably Florentine humours of Ghirlandaio (1449–94), in the chapel on the other side, whose cycle of episodes from the life of the Virgin is decidedly a case of 'the artist and friends' pictured within. Nor should you ignore the Spanish Chapel in the Chiostro Verde. Referred to as green after the prevailing tinge of its original frescoes, the dominant work here now is the huge omnium-gatherum painting on the chapel walls by Andrea da Firenze, begun in 1346 and finished a decade later. This cycle displays the essence of the fierce Dominican challenge to medieval life (the dogs, by the way, are the punning *domini canes* – 'dogs of the Lord'), St Thomas Aquinas, Church Militant and all, with astonishing energy.

What you must not miss, however, is the ancient monastic pharmacy, which, though the monks left it over a century ago, still trades from its original premises in Via della Scala at the further end of Piazza Santa Maria Novella. This is not the only one of its kind in Florence, yet in many respects it is the most attractive. Founded in the Middle Ages, it was the customary assemblage of stills, vats and bunches of dried herbs, but in the Renaissance it seems to have diversified into the cosmetic products on which its fame has since rested, though you can also buy that ghastly liqueur called Alkermes, sold in various sickly, syrupy forms in monasteries throughout Italy.

The vast hall in which the various unguents and essences are sold is a marvel of nineteenth-century design, in that pleasing neo-gothic idiom which goes with the operatic medievalism of Donizetti and Verdi, whose *Macbeth* had its first performance in 1847 in Florence, a year before this room was decorated. The ceiling is the original one belonging to the Acciaiuoli chapel, which this once was, but it was Enrico Romoli, designer of the beautiful walnut cabinets and counter, who commissioned Paolino Sarti to paint the charming little fresco panels of the four continents in the vault. Next door is an older pharmacy, dating from 1755, its cupboards crammed with chemists' equipment and a collection of those wonderful yellow-and-blue-patterned majolica jars made at Montelupo, west of Florence. There is also a room with portraits of the monks who supervised the business.

If you turn left out of the square, down the agreeably-named Via delle Belle Donne and Via del Trebbio, you reach Via de' Tornabuoni, one of the smartest and most sedate of Florentine thoroughfares, with Giuliano da San Gallo's splendid Palazzo Antinori at this end, and Palazzo Strozzi, the quintessential renaissance palace, half-way down, though you get the best view of it from the square round the corner. It was built to designs by Benedetto da Maiano (1442–97) in 1489, the foundation stone being carefully laid at sunrise according to a precise astrological forecast of the propitious hour. Much of the building's impact derives from its fearless, deliberate uncouthness: Filippo Strozzi chose this rusticated stonework so as not to antagonize Lorenzo de' Medici by any hint of overweening grandeur. The result is that, ironically, Palazzo Strozzi is the one secular building in Florence which invariably leaps to mind as archetypal of its period and locality.

At the bottom of Via de' Tornabuoni, you can either go straight on towards the river or turn left in search of more medieval and renaissance *palazzi*. If you choose the latter, Via Porta Rossa brings you to Palazzo Davanzati, an intriguing fusion of the old Guelph-versus-Ghibelline urban fortress with the gentler ordinances of a sixteenth-century palace, now converted into a fascinating museum of domestic life among the Florentine merchant aristocracy who brought wealth to the city. The staircase up through the narrow central courtyard gives on to a series of rambling family quarters, storerooms, a notable number of bench-hole lavatories, kitchens and a great bedroom decked out with curtains cunningly painted in fresco. I begin to sound like an estate agent, but the place really does possess a curious sense of being still lived in by medieval owners, who have simply run away and hidden for the day and will take over once more when the last visitor, with his camera and postcards, has shut the door and gone.

Go straight on, along what is essentially the southern side of the old Roman city, laid out to a grid plan rather maddeningly devised at an angle to the river. Eventually you reach Via Condotta, containing one of the city's best bookshops and a perfumery where you can mix your own essences. Across the north side of Piazza San Firenze from here lies the former town gaol, the Bargello, a little castle built in 1255 to house the administration of justice by the *podestà* or chief magistrate (the meaning of *bargello*). The place was both a prison and a refuge, and its grim associations continued until the last days of the Grand Dukes. Criminals were beheaded beside the well in the courtyard, and the Austrians, who occupied the city after the revolution of 1848, shot political prisoners here. It is a political image, indeed, that I want you to see, though the collection of renaissance sculptural masterpieces here is equally eloquent on religious and mythological themes. Donatello's diffident, gawky marble *David* of 1408, for example, hardly finds an echo in the insolent confidence of the same subject handled in bronze two decades later. Cellini, Giambologna and Sansovino are all here, and the sheer range of form and technique is more dramatically exposed than in any other Florentine museum.

If there is one sculpture, however, which for me answers one of those absurd questions along the lines of 'What luxury item would you take to your desert island?', it is the bust of Brutus by Michelangelo, in the gallery to the right of the entrance. This exceptional work, the more powerful for being unfinished, was probably carried out around 1540, when the artist's hopes for the defeat of Medicean tyranny had been thwarted with the seizure of power by Cosimo I. Marcus Junius Brutus, who expelled the Tarquins from Rome, thus became the tutelary spirit of political liberty down the ages.

The force of this icon and its proclamation of inalienable freedom through the surfaces, hollows and curves which reflect the controlling energy of the sculptor's chisel are incontestable. Is there a defiance in the eyes and in the hint of a smile governing the mouth, or is this a more visionary gaze? Most beautiful of all are the modelling of the facial bone structure and the sense of resistless power in the sinews of the neck. The *David*, with his over-large hands and gormless smirk, seems almost loutish beside it.

When you have gazed your fill at the Bargello, walk down through Piazza San Firenze (not a canonization of Florence, but a dedication to Saint Florentia) past the back of Palazzo Vecchio and the Uffizi. On the corner of Piazza dei Giudici overlooking the Arno is the Museo di Storia della Scienza, where even those without scientific interests will enjoy the handsome instruments displayed here. The tolerant rule of the Grand Dukes made for good relations with Protestant powers such as England, where dogma was not allowed to interfere with research into astronomy,

The snout of the Porcellino, the bronze boar in Florence's Mercato Nuovo, has been rubbed smooth by people touching it for luck.

natural history and medicine. Several members of the ducal family over various generations became enthusiastic scientific amateurs, encouraging correspondence with foreign experts and, most notably in the case of Galileo, shielding native adepts from the misguided zeal of Rome.

The lens through which Galileo observed Jupiter's satellites is here and so is the magnet he presented to Ferdinand II, whose Accademia del Cimento, a scientific research society founded in 1657, provided the basis of the collection. There are wonderful shagreen-covered telescopes, sextants, armillary spheres, early microscopes and burning glasses, and a fascinating ancestor of the modern calculator, devised by the seventeenth-century English mathematician Sir

PIAZZA
DELLA SIGNORIA

Samuel Morland. The most gruesome of the exhibits is the collection of eighteenth-century wax models demonstrating the various phases of pregnancy and childbirth, with nothing omitted.

So as to avoid this part of the Lungarno (as the road following the river is called), which is noisy and overcrowded, go back and turn left into Piazza della Signoria (which, at the height of the tourist season, may seem no improvement). Crossing Via Por Santa Maria and going down Via delle Terme brings you to Piazza Santa Trinita, where the granite column in the middle was a gift from the Pope, who took it from the Roman baths of Caracalla, to Cosimo I in 1564. According to a sad tale, a servant girl in a nearby palace was executed for stealing a rope of pearls, which was later discovered in the scales of the figure of Justice on top of the pillar, where it had been hidden by a jackdaw.

Santa Trinita itself is enjoyable, for the mystic darkness of its fourteenth-century interior, where the votive candles burn all the more dramatically, and for the limpid grace of the Virgin greeted by a many-hued Archangel in the *Annunciation* by Lorenzo Monaco (1370–1425) forming the altarpiece of the Bartolini Salimbeni chapel. Also seek out the tomb of Benozzo Federighi, Bishop of Fiesole, to the left of the choir, an outstanding work by Luca della Robbia, particularly in its rendering of what one Victorian writer diplomatically calls 'the admirably truthful figure of the dead bishop'.

Ghirlandaio is here too, sprightly, inventive and colourful as ever, in the frescoes of the life of St Francis adorning the Sassetti chapel on the other side of the

The often-reproduced features of Cosimo I, seen here in a fine statue by Giambologna in Piazza della Signoria, Florence.

choir. They were painted for a rich merchant and his wife, whose portraits flank the altar, between 1482 and 1485. *The Death of St Francis* is generally accounted the best, but I like the episode which shows the saint bringing a child of the Spini family to life again. The little boy sits up, keen as mustard, on top of his bier, while his mother praises God, watched by groups of sumptuously garbed patricians. Each is a recognizable contemporary portrait, for the miracle happened in Florence some two centuries before Ghirlandaio painted the fresco, and you can see Santa Trinita's old façade in the background, with the bridge beyond.

Across the Ponte Santa Trinita, a fine reconstruction of the original destroyed in 1944, lies the part of the city where most of us would like to live. Oltrarno – 'beyond the Arno' – has a wholly distinctive atmosphere, inherited from its beginnings in the early Middle Ages as a fortified outwork to which the townsfolk could retreat for safety. Nowadays it is an area in which the palaces of noble families like the Frescobaldi and the Capponi rub shoulders with the German Institute, the Anglican church, workshops making fake antiques and the flats of myriad art historians, both impecunious and well-heeled.

The further west you go, the less tourist-conscious this area grows. Its restaurants, especially around the Carmine and San Frediano, are less fancy, more genuinely Florentine, and the meaning of the Italian word *popolare*, more than just 'of the people', is readily grasped. To savour this atmosphere walk down Via Maggio from the bridge and take a sharp right turn into Piazza Santo Spirito, the kind of Italian town square of which Florence possesses all too few. Here an old *palazzo* with a *pensione* on top, a fountain and a vegetable market are presided over by the façade of Brunelleschi's church at one end, waiting for ever to be given its marble facing.

Brunelleschi died in 1446, soon after the building of Santo Spirito had begun. The final project, far less

27

ambitious than his original idea, was tampered with after his death, but the interior, with its mass of semicircular chapels like the pleatings of a dress, makes the true 'frozen music' of architecture, holding the renaissance spirit more perfectly than many other places in Florence. No wonder Brunelleschi's pupil Antonio Manetti called it 'a beautiful thing which had no peer in Christendom'. Giuliano da Sangallo's sacristy, added in 1489, was one of the more tactful and effective additions to the initial design.

A good plan at this point would be to walk westwards to look at Masaccio's Brancacci chapel frescoes in the church of the Carmine, but if you are turning east and retracing your steps towards the rather unpleasant area around the Ponte Vecchio, make sure, when you reach the approach to the bridge, that you go right and into the little square where the church of Santa Felicita stands. The church itself, built by Ferdinando Ruggieri in 1736, is elegant without a hint of pomposity, incorporating chapels from an earlier building and the special stalls for the grand-ducal family, who arrived for worship via a corridor designed by Vasari joining nearby Palazzo Pitti to the Uffizi.

In the Capponi chapel, on your right as you enter the church, is an astonishing *Deposition* by Jacopo Pontormo (1494–1557), a scene in which the unearthly remoteness of the participants is emphasized by the livid pallor of their flesh and their immense, unseeing eyes. To the right is his *Annunciation*, a poetic fantasy with the protagonists separated by the masonry of the altar: Gabriel averts his face, but the Virgin turns with a preoccupied stare, as if he had broken in upon a mystical exercise she was loth to interrupt.

The Ponte Vecchio, most venerable of Florentine bridges, dating from the fourteenth century.

Climbing the hill from Santa Felicita takes you up the Costa di San Giorgio into a suddenly rural stillness, through which you can wander, with increasing enchantment, towards Arcetri, where Galileo spent his last years and Tchaikovsky wrote his string sextet *Souvenir de Florence*, a powerful mingling of Italy and Russia. If you turn left along Via di Belvedere, however, you will eventually reach Porta San Miniato, from which steps flanked by Stations of the Cross take you up to the church with its superb view over the city, here spread before you in a prospect which has not substantially changed in five hundred years.

San Miniato al Monte must be one of the best-loved churches in Italy, for its position, that of an eyecatcher in the Florentine townscape, for the beauty and delicacy of its black, green and white marble façade, and for the potent sense of untroubled placidity which it radiates. The whole creation represents a flawless synthesis between its original romanesque structure and the adornments of sculpture, ceramic decoration and painting lavished on it by the Medici during the fifteenth century. The harmony of these is complete, and the eye delights as much in Michelozzo's Cappella del Crocifisso, an entrancing little tabernacle with an arched roof decorated by Luca della Robbia, as in the chapel of San Jacopo, built to commemorate Dom Jaime, the saintly nephew of King Alfonso of Portugal, who died aged 26, already a cardinal, in 1459. The design of the chapel combines the talents of Antonio Manetti, Luca della Robbia and Antonio Rossellino (1427–79), creator of the imposing tomb itself, in a decorative scheme of matchless refinement.

At the turn of the present century, as a foreign visitor, you might have been armed with introductions to owners of the villas on the ridge of Bellosguardo, or gone somewhat further afield, calling, perhaps, on the eccentric Janet Ross at Poggio Gherardo, who could engage you on anything from the lives of the early Medici to the secrets of Tuscan vegetable cookery, or on Lady Sybil Cutting at Villa Medici, whose daughter Iris Origo is one of the most valuable modern interpreters of Italy to English-speaking readers.

Villa Medici itself, built by Cosimo il Vecchio around 1458, sits on the hill east of Florence which is crowned by the little town of Fiesole. Actually it is not much more than a village, with hardly anything to recall its importance as Etruscan and Roman Faesulae, since the medieval Florentines wiped away most of it so as to blot out any potential threat to the city below. There are bronzes, urns and sculptural fragments from the Etruscan period in the elegantly porticoed museum above the fine Roman theatre dating from the reign of Augustus, nowadays an ideal setting for open-air performances during the summer months. That this was part of a sort of 'entertainment complex' is shown by the baths next to the theatre, built about a century later.

From here there is an outstanding prospect east down the steep ridge on which Fiesole is built. Back in the main square you can look at the *duomo*, whose monumental romanesque interior embraces a chapel to the right of the choir containing the tomb of Bishop Leonardo Salutati, who died in 1462. Salutati came from one of the richest Florentine families, which commissioned Mino da Fiesole (1431–84) to create a monument in which grandeur was to be outmatched by truth to nature in the rendition of the bishop's features. Mino had known Salutati well, having carried out, at his direction, the altar of the Madonna with Christ and St John which stands opposite the tomb itself.

Climb the hill to what was the ancient citadel, a site now occupied by the convent of San Francesco, with

---

Steps to the church of San Miniato al Monte, dramatically placed on a hilltop overlooking Florence.

little cloisters round which you can wander freely and a thoroughly bizarre museum in which travelling friars of the past have flung in everything from stuffed fish to Chinese scrolls. Ruskin once stood on the terrace outside the convent and was moved to lapidary prose by the view, with its 'terraced gardens . . . showing at intervals through their framework of rich leaf and rubied flower the far away-bends of the Arno beneath its slope of olive'.

As you descend towards Florence, the road leads past the convent of San Domenico, where, as one early biographer puts it, 'Fra Angelico gathered in abundance the flowers of art which he seemed to have plucked from Paradise.' The only flowers he left behind here are a *Virgin Enthroned with Angels and Saints*, painted in 1430 before the artist went to live and work at San Marco, and two frescoes in the chapter-house. Beyond San Domenico is the Badia Fiesolana, Cosimo de' Medici's rebuilding of an ancient church dating from the days of St Romulus, Fiesole's first bishop, ordained by St Paul himself. The abbey's conventual buildings are now a university.

To the south of the city, easily seen from the motorways to Arezzo and Siena, is the Certosa, the great Charterhouse of Galluzzo, founded in 1342 for the Carthusian Order by the powerful banker Niccolò Acciaiuoli. Though the Order no longer administers it, the place is still a monastery, sheltering a group of Cistercian monks whose friendliness and good humour is far removed from the dour image projected by their medieval counterparts.

The Certosa is an immense, rambling complex of cloisters and chapels, dating from Acciaiuoli's original foundation to the early nineteenth century. Of the earlier parts, the most beautiful is the large cloister, with its 18 cells, little houses from which each brother emerges only for divine service and communal meals. Over the cloister arches runs an extraordinary series of roundels containing glazed terracotta busts represent-

The meeting between King Victor Emmanuel and Garibaldi at Teano, a statuary group in the main square at Fiesole.

ing saints and biblical figures, the work of Giovanni della Robbia. You should also look at the chapter-house, with its vividly characterized effigy, on the floor, of Leonardo Buonafe, bishop of Cortona, who died in 1545, by Francesco di Giuliano da Sangallo, at the monastery church, with its wealth of late renaissance decoration in the choir-stalls, ceiling frescoes and altar statuary, and at a hauntingly impressive cycle of four paintings by the Sienese artist Rutilio Manetti (1571–1639), which shows Carthusians in acts of devotion. The set of lunettes of the Passion by Pontormo in the picture gallery is, alas, almost irrecoverably damaged by humidity.

Finally, if you feel genuinely adventurous, leave Florence by the old Via Bolognese, north-east towards the Apennines, the road by which eighteenth-century milords and Victorians in search of the picturesque used to arrive in Tuscany, and still lined with splendid villas as it climbs the steep hillside. Just beyond Pratolino, where the Villa Demidoff occupies what was merely the pages' quarters of a colossal rustic pleasure-dome built for Bianca Cappello by her lover Grand Duke Francesco I, turn right and start the tortuous ascent towards the sanctuary of Monte Senario.

Practically no guide to Tuscany mentions this delightful spot, which is a pity, for the conventual buildings are pleasantly theatrical, with steps rising to a pretty little rococo basilica with stuccoed angels and much gilding, and there is a fascinating sequence of hermitages on the way up the hill. The convent was founded by the so-called Seven Saints of the Greater Company of Holy Mary in 1241, who instituted the order known as the Servites. Their desire for seclusion was amply gratified at Monte Senario, which you should visit early on a summer morning if you can, so that you can enjoy what is surely the most amazing view in all Tuscany from the broad terrace at the back of the monastery. From here, the great sequence of indented valleys to the north, known as the Mugello, spreads itself like a huge patterned cornice, an invitation to go down the hill and begin your Tuscan journey.

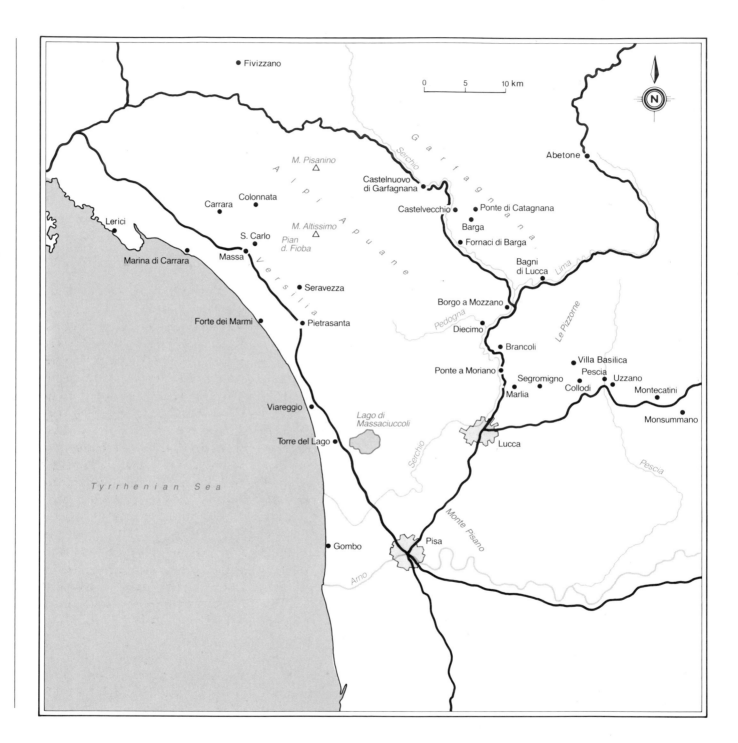

1
Lucca and the Garfagnana

Lucca – Pescia – Montecatini – Bagni di Lucca –
Barga – Castelnuovo – Massa – Carrara –
Viareggio

Tuscany's history holds up a mirror to Italy herself. The pattern of small states chequering the peninsula before the drive for unity during the nineteenth century is echoed in the amazing variety of 'thrones, dominations, lordships, princedoms, powers' within a single area. Whole sections of what we now think of as Tuscan territory only came under the centralized government of Florence during the last days of the Grand Dukes, and in some areas the political arrangement was of a wondrous and enduring complexity.

Perhaps this explains why the north-western corner of the province always feels different in ways not merely connected with landscape. It was shared, after all, by four different rulers. The valleys of the mountainous Garfagnana region belonged to the Duchy of Modena, which later took over the territory of Massa and Carrara after an advantageous marriage with the last of their reigning family. The towns of Barga, Pietrasanta and Fivizzano were Florentine, and several other cities paid homage to the Hapsburg Emperor. The whole of the rest was the domain of the only state which Florence, among its near neighbours, had never managed to crush, the little republic of Lucca.

There is something admirable in the tenacity of the *lucchesi* in clutching hold of their independence, and not for nothing are they noted among Tuscans for their passionate *campanilismo*, a loyalty to their city and its surrounding countryside. Pious and politically rather conservative, they validate all those blush-making clichés used by guidebook writers about 'a proud people', though perhaps this also explains why they are not specially willing to see what is still a working provincial capital turned into yet another tourist trap. The foreign expatriates who live in the area, Tuscany's most sophisticated and ruthlessly critical, are equally reluctant to watch it go the way of Pisa or Siena: 'Don't write about Lucca,' one of them told me, 'it'll make people want to visit it.'

I should find it hard to put anybody off. For a start, the place has, more than anywhere else I know in Europe, an extraordinary, almost tangible savour of age. It has not consumed, digested and discarded experience like other cities, but taken it on board as a vital, unchanging feature of a complex organism. Practically every street, for example, contains a romanesque church (nearly always locked, alas), which appears to have grown solidly and irremovably into the mass of houses around it, with none of that

St Martin, one of Lucca's patron saints, shown here in the act of blessing the city.

vulnerable quality such buildings might possess elsewhere.

This air of relentless permanence, so opposed to the Italian obsession with novelty, is sealed by the embrace of the city walls, a moated, brick-built girdle of ramparts and towers, begun in the mid sixteenth century on medieval foundations and completed a hundred years later. With one exception the eleven bastions are all named after Lucca's patron saints, and were once crowned with cannon until the Austrians carried them off in 1799. Soon afterwards, when Lucca became a duchy under a branch of the Spanish Bourbons, the court architect Lorenzo Nottolini (1787–1851) transformed the ramparts into a delectable circular avenue of lime trees under which

generations of *lucchesi* have strolled and dallied, between *'Lucca dentro e Lucca fuori'* – 'Lucca within and Lucca without'.

The city gates, suitably stately and mostly contemporaneous with the walls, are neither more nor less than little palaces. In 1812, when the neighbouring River Serchio flooded the plain, they were hermetically sealed, and Napoleon's sister Elisa Baciocchi, ruler of the state, had to be winched over the walls by a special crane. It is from her own gate, the Porta Elisa of 1804, that you enter Lucca from the direction of Florence. At the top of her eponymous street is what remains of the old town ditch of the medieval city, whose growth from the original Roman square plan is clearly seen on the map. The archway beyond is a lone survivor from some earlier walls, and the presence of others even older is marked by the church of Santa Maria Forisportam ('outside the gate').

This, the church which Ruskin claimed first inspired him to study medieval architecture, gives visitors their first taste of Lucchese romanesque, which, although heavily marked by Pisan influence, makes maximum impact here through its sheer abundance. The façade, dating from the late twelfth century, plays freely with contrasted arcading and heavily incised diamond-shaped recesses above the doorways. Opposite Santa Maria, in the Palazzo Penitesi, lived the French essayist Michel de Montaigne, whose engrossing journal of his Italian tour in 1580–1 documents his search for good health and his brushes with such illustrious or notorious contemporaries as the poet Torquato Tasso and Bianca Cappello. From here you can turn down the Via della Rosa towards the botanical gardens, another of Elisa Baciocchi's numberless gifts to her realm. These are

An arcade in Via Elisa, Lucca.

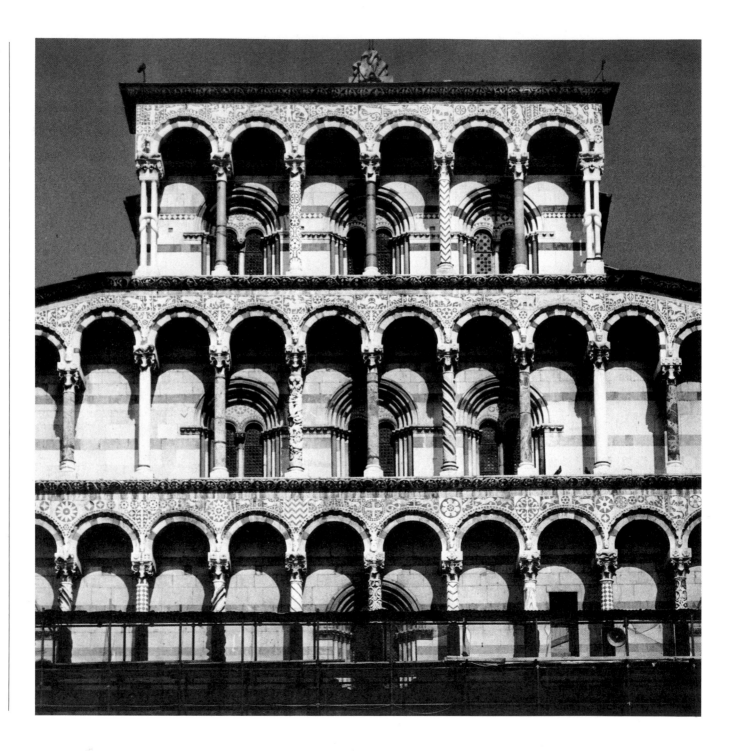

now most enterprisingly laid out by their enthusiastic superintendents as a living museum of Tuscan flora, displaying species from mountains and hills to coastal plain.

To see a purer form of Lucchese romanesque, go left up the lane off Via della Rosa and confront the blatant handsomeness of San Martino, the cathedral church. This is a mixture of twelfth-century work – in the porch, upper façade (missing its topmost storey) and looming battlemented campanile – with various gothic additions, notably in the buttressing of the north side of the nave. The surrounds of all three doors are decorated with excellent sculptured reliefs: the Deposition and Nativity scenes embellishing the left-hand entrance, attributed to Nicola Pisano, make a stark contrast with the martyrdom of St Regulus (falling under a blow from a nonchalant-looking Goth) and his dispute with the Arian heretics. These are probably by a sculptor known as Maestro Lombardo, who also executed the panels of the twelve months, without which no Italian romanesque cathedral was complete.

Inside is the customary mystical gloom, in which it comes as something of a surprise to discover a Tintoretto hanging above an altar in the south aisle, one of the very few works by this Venetian painter to adorn a church outside his native city. A specially commissioned *Last Supper*, it was painted around 1592 and is full of the artist's typical light-out-of-darkness effects. The best pictures elsewhere in the cathedral are the excellent Ghirlandaio altarpiece in the sacristy, a *Virgin and Child with Saints*, and the same subject as handled by Fra Bartolomeo (1475–1517), with his usual vapoury lightness of brushwork, in the chapel to the far left of the high altar.

Decorated arcading on the façade of Lucca's cathedral of San Martino.

A little beyond this, in the north transept, the noble lady Ilaria del Carretto lies in marmoreal stillness on top of the tomb chest prepared for her by her mourning husband Paolo Guinigi, around which a train of dolorous *putti* drape heavy swags of flowers and leaves. She died in 1405, and it was Jacopo della Quercia (1367–1438) who created this serene image of conjugal fidelity, underlining its message with the lugubrious mastiff puppy crouched at Ilaria's feet. Recently damaged by a maniac, the effigy has been expertly repaired.

Paolo, tyrant of Lucca, may not have been noted for probity or mildness, but like all other *lucchesi* of his day, he was devoted to the *Volto Santo*, the Holy Face of Lucca, a miraculous wooden figure of Christ which is kept in its domed tabernacle in the nave, designed by Matteo Civitali (1436–1501). The sculpture is said to have been carved in cedar wood by the New Testament figure Nicodemus, his hands guided by angels, and to have floated to Italy from Palestine. Revered throughout Europe – by the French as 'Saint Vaudeluc' and by the Germans as 'Die Heilige Kummerniss' – it attracted hordes of pilgrims annually, and King William Rufus of England used to swear his most formidable oaths 'by the Holy Face of Lucca'. Its translation is celebrated on 13 September, when the image is dressed in special robes and there is a procession through the streets of the city, though experts now believe it to have been carved by a Lombard master during the ninth century. There is certainly a strong touch of the Germanic warrior hero about the face, with its bristling moustachios, and readers of Anglo-Saxon poetry will be reminded of a similar presentation of Christ in *The Dream of the Rood*.

Lucca's earliest cathedral was the church of San Giovanni on the north side of Via Duomo. Though substantially restored in 1622, several romanesque and gothic features have survived, including a baptistery with a conical dome of 1393, and a doorway of

Above **Duchess Maria Luisa, benefactress of Lucca, by the great nineteenth-century Florentine sculptor Lorenzo Bartolini.**

Left **Christ hands the keys of his church to St Peter, a stucco relief from Lucca.**

particoloured marbles with a sculpted frieze of the Twelve Apostles, similar in style to that of the *duomo* itself.

From here it is a short step towards a different, though no less crucial aspect of Lucca's history. The square known as the Piazza Napoleone is really a synthesis of the good intentions of the city's rulers towards its people, for, whatever the failings of the aristocratic republican oligarchy, or of Elisa Baciocchi and the Duchess Maria Luisa (and these were many), their attachment to Lucca itself was never in doubt. Bartolini's statue of the Duchess, a bigoted Spaniard whose morbidly suspicious snooping made her heartily disliked by her subjects, faces the palace Lorenzo Nottolini began rebuilding for her in 1818. In fact Nottolini's task, carried out with typical refinement, was to modernize and extend a renaissance structure created by the Florentine Bartolomeo Ammanati (1511–92) in 1576, after the explosion of a powder magazine had destroyed the original seat of municipal government. Since the city is still ruled from here, visitors are not generally admitted, but if there is an exhibition in the state apartments, try to get a glimpse of Ammanati's loggia in the central courtyard and Nottolini's staircase and sculpture gallery, fit for the rustling bombazines of the devout duchess and her starchy court. Also, look at the west side of the palace, dating from 1724, sometimes attributed to one of my favourite Italian architects, Filippo Juvarra (1676–1736), a Sicilian best known for his work in Piedmont.

A capital city must have a theatre, a need admirably filled here by the Teatro del Giglio on the south side of the square, an accomplished essay in neo-classicism by Giovanni Lazzarini (1817). This is one of many opera houses which the newly-restored Italian rulers erected around this time as temples of legitimism, where the sovereign could be worshipped in the velvet and gilt shrine of a royal box. This one is not used as much as it should be: a short Puccini season and a few concerts are a good deal less than it, or Lucca, deserve, particularly as this is Puccini's birthplace. You can see the house where he was born in 1858 in the Via di Poggio, left out of Via Veneto off the Piazza Napoleone. An equally talented and influential *lucchese* composer spent his childhood on the other side of Piazza San Michele, into which the street debouches. Luigi Boccherini (1743–1805) is now known only for a handful of chamber works, but his symphonies, quartets and concertos were highly praised in their day, and he was one of the very few masters whom Mozart, not noted for generosity to his contemporaries, was willing to take seriously. He spent much of his later life in Spain, whose dance rhythms powerfully marked his style. Eighteenth-century Lucca sent forth more than one footloose musician: the flautist and oboist Francesco Barsanti gave his best years to Edinburgh, delighting the Scots with his folksong settings and improvisations on reel and strathspey tunes.

You are now at the heart of Lucca, half-way along the city's east-west main drag consisting of three or four streets laid end to end, lined with shops and bars and an eternal witness to the vitality of an Italian provincial town. The civilized habit of shutting up shop during the afternoon and opening again at four o'clock means that these narrow lanes are at their busiest in the early evening, loud with gregarious, gossiping strollers. There is an Italian word for this, which I would like to introduce into English, *formicolare* – literally, 'to be like an ant-hill'. The sight and sound of streets formiculating with busy Tuscans is pleasanter than it might at first seem.

The façade of the church in the Piazza San Michele is yet another stunning essay in romanesque, the decorated arcading made more ornate by the black and white marble friezes of animals and birds above the successive rows of arches. Much of this is in fact

Above **This clock at Lucca dates from the city's brief nineteenth-century spell as the capital of an independent duchy.**

Right **Romanesque exuberance characterizes the church of San Michele in Foro at Lucca.**

cunning nineteenth-century restoration, and if you look carefully you can distinguish representations of Garibaldi, Victor Emmanuel and Cavour, the architects of Italian unification, among the 'medieval' corbel heads. Follow Via Calderia north of here past the church of Sant'Agostino, whose campanile incorporates the remains of a large Roman theatre, the layout of which has clearly influenced the alignment of

Left **The superb gardens of Palazzo Controni-Pfanner, Lucca, were laid out in the seventeenth century, perhaps by Filippo Juvarra. They include lichen-spotted marble deities, such as this statue of Juno as patron goddess of marriage** (*above*).

baroque garden, laid out perhaps by Filippo Juvarra himself.

The purest and plainest of Lucca's larger romanesque churches stands in a long open space at the end of Via Cesare Battisti. It is dedicated to San Frediano, one of those heroic Irish wanderers who carried Christianity across Dark Age Europe and died here in the late sixth century as a much revered pastor, when the city was capital of the Longobard marquisate of Tuscia. The austere colonnaded basilica is entered through doors which look like narrow holes in an equally stark façade, unadorned except by a much restored thirteenth-century mosaic of Christ in glory. The apse and high altar are strikingly bare of decoration and the pillars are taken from Roman Lucca, outside whose walls San Frediano founded his church.

Three romanesque sculptors worked on the font, though only one of them has left us his name in the inscription *Me fecit Robertus magister in arte peritus –* 'Robert made me, an accomplished master of his art'. Not nearly as accomplished as his colleague, who carved the forthright, energetic scenes from the life of Moses around the bowl, for me among the most compelling achievements of their period.

Comparably forceful, in a different epoch and context, is the fresco cycle covering the chapel of Sant'Agostino in the north aisle. This is by the Bolognese painter Amico Aspertini (1474–1552), dated 1508–9, and the scenes include episodes from Lucca's religious past, with portraits of the chief citizens, developed in a style wholly alien to the smooth concords, demure countenances and decorous blendings of his contemporaries. This is northern Italian art, shot through with allusions to Flanders and Germany, full of ugly, knobbly, goggle-eyed faces, abundantly characterful in their coarseness. No wonder the great art historian Roberto Longhi called this painter 'an authentic discoverer of new lands'.

On the other side of the church, in a chapel

surrounding houses and streets. Beyond, in Via Cesare Battisti, is Palazzo Controni-Pfanner, an imposing patrician house of 1667, with an ample sweep of staircase and loggia to the principal reception rooms of the *piano nobile*. Here a permanent array of eighteenth- and nineteenth-century costume from the aristocracy of republic and duchy is seen against a backdrop of fresco decoration by Pietro Scorzini (*c.*1720). Between the *palazzo* and the ramparts, an enchanting sweep of clipped bay hedges, trim gravel walks, lemon trees in pots and lichen-spotted marble deities make up a dedicated to her, lies St Zita, who died in Lucca in 1278. She spent all her life as a maidservant in a noble family, who revered her for her holiness, and in 1952 she was officially declared the patroness of chambermaids. The Lucca she knew was still enclosed within its Roman ramparts, and it is towards a singular Roman survival that the Via Fillungo now takes you. The amphitheatre at Lucca is probably the only such structure to have been preserved simply by people dwelling inside it. Thanks to the surrounding houses having been dismantled by Nottolini in 1830–9, the outer shell is now laid bare and you can walk round the entire oval both inside and out and see how the fabric, pierced by four gateways, has been gently absorbed by a ring of tall houses. This used to be a lively fruit and vegetable market, but its destiny, oddly similar to London's Covent Garden, has been that of turning what Italians call *una zona popolare* – a working-class area – into a fancy array of shops and apartments, misguided and irresponsible though this initiative may seem.

The city's western end is dominated by the memory of the Guinigi family, whose palace stands on the north-western corner of Via Sant'Andrea. Built in the late fourteenth century, it represents one of the finest statements of domestic gothic architecture in this part of Tuscany, with its triple and quadruple groups of ogival windows under broad-spanned brick arches, and its tall machicolated tower, on top of which a clump of trees has sprouted for as long as anybody can recall.

The Guinigi's star sank almost as soon as it rose, in the person of Ilaria del Carretto's husband, the overweening Paolo, ultimately crushed in the Florentine-Milanese power struggles of the 1430s. It was he who built the Villa Guinigi as a pleasure palace outside the old medieval walls (turn right off Via dell'Angelo Custode into Piazza San Francesco). For its period, and indeed for what it is, the villa is historically fascinating – one has to travel as far as Ferrara to find anything exactly comparable – but its tremendous length and deadening uniformity, as well as the impression that the upper windows are squeezed in under the roof, give it the oppressive sameness of institutional architecture from a much later age. While still standing outside notice the plinth of the column to the Madonna dello Stellario in the piazza, a pleasing glimpse of seventeenth-century Lucca in sculptured relief.

Villa Guinigi houses the city art gallery, with everything from barbaric Longobard jewellery to works by the Civitali, that great *lucchese* family of fifteenth- and sixteenth-century carvers, marquetry workers and architects, and a set of lively panels by Vincenzo Consani (1818–87) for an unfinished monument to the Duchess Maria Luisa. I regret the absence of any truly representative pictures by Lucca's greatest painter, Pompeo Batoni (1708–87), whose portraits of English 'milords' on the Grand Tour executed in his studio in Rome are compositions of tremendous verve and sophistication, presenting a classic image of the noble connoisseur. The real Batoni is there, rather than in the chaste perfection of the various mythologies and saints which remain at Lucca itself.

To foreign travellers the republic of Lucca was, till the last, an object of mingled curiosity and scorn. Montaigne disapproved of the fact that it was protected by the Holy Roman Emperor, while the President de Brosses, whose mid eighteenth-century account of his Italian journey is shot through with Gallic contempt, thought the tiny state's very existence an absurdity. Another French writer, in 1788, criticized the harshness of a government which forbade women to wear jewels except at the carnival season, and Dr Johnson's friend Mrs Piozzi considered the place a byword for thoroughgoing stinginess. Still, the republic survived, with its little

Swiss guard and its various grand functionaries, including one whose sixty-day residence in the Palazzo Pubblico earned him the wonderful title of *Gonfaloniere delle sessanta minestre* – 'Gonfaloniere of the sixty soups'.

The nobles of the ruling oligarchy followed the customary practice of quitting the town in summer for their country retreats scattered along the hillsides of the Lucchesia, the fertile valley of the River Serchio. These villas and their surrounding countryside are unlike anything regarded as typically Tuscan by visitors from beyond the Alps. For a start, the soil hereabouts is exceptionally fertile, and the roads from Florence are lined with nurseries and market gardens, so that even the humblest peasant plot is green and fecund to bursting. The whole landscape has a softness and diversity which the staring cornlands of the *crete senesi* or the lurid sunflower fields of the Val di Chiana notably lack.

Village houses in the Lucchesia have their own style, basically built as tall blocks of dwellings bonded together around a courtyard. Each has its *fienile*, or hay barn, with windows of zigzagged bricks to aerate the drying winter fodder. In between the various communities, especially around the heights of Le Pizzorne north-east of Lucca, lie the villas, each surrounded by an ornate park fusing both Italian and English garden features, and each far more self-consciously a town dweller's rustic resort than any of the farmhouse fortresses of the Florentines and Sienese.

You can visit several of them by taking the main road north out of Lucca up the left bank of the Serchio, turning right to Marlia. This, the grandest pile of them all, is open solely at the whim of its owners, and you can count yourself lucky to be able to view the garden, but the place deserves more than a nod as a symbol of the region's Napoleonic destiny. It was here that Elisa Bonaparte and her complaisant spouse Felice Baciocchi

decided to turn the existing villa into a residence worthy of the vigorous, efficient and generally beneficent sway of the Princess of Piombino and her consort – as they had now become. Until chased away by a British expeditionary force, Elisa successfully played the *grande dame* here and dallied with the young Niccolò Paganini, whose legendary violin technique – at least according to him – used to make her swoon with emotion. As for poor Felice, he made the best of things, consoling himself with a sardonic play on his name, which in Italian means 'happy'. He had changed it from Pasquale, which in those days was synonymous with 'fool', so he used to say: 'When I was Pasquale then I was Felice: now I'm Felice, I've become Pasquale.'

From Marlia, go east towards Segromigno, where the Villa Mansi provides the perfect example of the gradual transmutations of a *lucchese* country house. The original building, probably a fairly simple late renaissance affair, was amplified by Muzio Oddi in 1635, who added the two flanking pavilions and the central loggia. It was further elaborated a century later by Gian Francesco Giusti, responsible for the balustrades and statues which add the desired touches of pomp. The garden is something of a mess: Filippo Juvarra's original plans were substantially altered in the nineteenth century and recent owners have made further questionable changes.

Much more beautiful, because less manicured and scrubbed, is Villa Torrigiani, just a couple of kilometres to the south of Camigliano. This is approached by a grand avenue between the flanking houses of a model village, built by an eighteenth-century member of the family who, having been the republic's ambassador to France, liked to refer to his newly-created hamlet as Parigi (Paris). Although similar to Villa Mansi in its deeply recessed portico and wealth of presiding statuary (the architect was probably Oddi again), the design of Villa Torrigiani is

47

more imaginative in the way its three storeys seem to recede towards the central belvedere. When the owners are not in residence, the bailiff's wife will take you through the cheerfully frescoed saloons, furnished with whatever has survived a series of burglaries. The gardens, mossy and unkempt, are a joy, especially the stretch at the back of the house, seen from beneath the broad arcade of the loggia.

Joining the road towards Pescia and then turning sharp north will bring you to the most fanciful villa garden, at Collodi, more famous as the birthplace of Carlo Lorenzini, better known as Carlo Collodi (1826–90), the creator of *Pinocchio*, one of Italy's few memorable children's books. On top of the steep hillside perches Villa Garzoni, whose austere grandeur created in the early years of the eighteenth century is attributed to Filippo Juvarra. You will need a full purse to enter house and grounds: the entrance fee is grossly extortionate but worth the sting for a glimpse of the frescoed rooms and, most of all, for the great fall of terraced gardens, among Italy's most ambitious, laid out in 1786–7 by Ottaviano Diodati. The fame this single creation brought him spread well beyond the *lucchesi*, and he contributed major articles on gardening to an edition of the great French *Encyclopedie*.

This is a 'feature' garden, in which the wanderer is continually arrested by humour or novelty in the design, along lines similar to those being tried by Diodati's English contemporaries at Rousham and Stourhead. Having, for instance, been splashed by concealed fountains, you could have taken a bath in earnest at the *romitorio* (hermitage) at the top of the hill, to the accompaniment of music provided by hidden performers, or simply strayed down the flights of steps from parterre to parterre among the hedges and statues.

Back on the main road, plunge down towards Pescia in its valley. The town may not at first look especially prepossessing – a long, narrow, grubby place without much character – but there is actually a good deal here to enjoy if you are ready to seek it out. The apparently unpromising church of San Francesco, at the principal crossroads, contains the earliest notable painting of the saint in its south aisle. The work of Bonaventura Berlinghieri, who both signed and dated his canvas, it was painted in 1235, only nine years after Francis's death. The tall, linear icon is surrounded by scenes from his life, but its effect has recently been spoilt by the worst kind of cosmetic restoration.

Crossing the foul, garbage-choked torrent that is the River Pescia into the claustrophobic Piazza Mazzini at the centre of town, you should park here and walk northwards into Via Cairoli, where an almost imperceptible sign on the door of the municipal library in Palazzo Galeotti ushers you up a humble flight of stairs into the civic museum.

Most of the galleries of northern Italy have had money spent on them in recent years, but Pescia has mercifully escaped, retaining – for how much longer? – the dusty, haphazard quality it must have had from its very foundation. I love this kind of display more than any other, since you never quite know what you will find. Here, among the crusts labelled 'follower of' and 'school of', are a *Madonna* by Lorenzo Monaco and an *Annunciation* by Bicci di Lorenzo (1373–1452). Or is it by Lorenzo di Bicci, who lived at the same time? It honestly does not matter much, as the guide mumbles over the catalogue, leading you through what are essentially the early nineteenth-century rooms of a not very rich noble family's palace, veiled in cobwebby gloom.

For me the most exciting part of the museum, largely because it is wholly unexpected, is the section

---

The seventeenth-century façade of Villa Torrigiani at Camigliano, north of Lucca.

commemorating the operatic composer Giovanni Pacini (1797–1867). In his time this prolific artist was as successful as Verdi or Donizetti, and though without the genius of either, he had a crude originality which they both admired. His success was partly due to his phenomenal effect on women. As a young man he became Pauline Borghese's lover, and in his mature years he took up with the powerful Milanese hostess Countess Samoyloff. Born in Sicily, he settled in a handsome villa near Pescia and left his fortune to the town, whose theatre is named after him. In the museum his manuscript scores are simply scattered about on top of the piano for anybody to pick up.

Before you leave Pescia, it is worth sampling the fare at Cecco, in Viale Forti by the river, one of the less pretentious, more serious Tuscan restaurants, widely respected in the region for dishes such as *pollastrino* (chicken cooked with lemon and garlic under a terracotta brick), and a delicious soup made with *funghi porcini* and catmint. Now, for digestion's sake, climb the slope to Uzzano, an immensely attractive old village on a hill to the east, with a tremendous view down to the distant ridges above the Arno across a plain glinting with greenhouses, full of the carnations for which Pescia is noted.

Return to the main road and penetrate the sprawling spa town of Montecatini. This is an essential Tuscan experience, whether you like it or not, if only because of the bizarre atmosphere such places invariably give off. The curative properties of the five sulphur springs have been enjoyed since the Middle Ages, but it was only during the late eighteenth century, when adequate drainage and proper accommodation for the bathers were installed, that the spa's reputation was confirmed.

A Tuscan roofscape of vivid red tiles at Pescia.

Palatial grandeur welcomes bathers at the fashionable spa of Montecatini.

England is alone among European nations in failing to take water cures seriously: in Italy, as in France or Germany, spas continue to thrive, as proved by the yearly pilgrimage of invalids to Montecatini, to submit themselves to mud-baths, douches and drenches under proper medical supervision. The whole place has that peculiar spa atmosphere of controlled tranquillity and slightly strained repose, with clusters of sedate hotels amid its lawns and avenues. Its architecture, especially that of the baths themselves, scattered across a broad park in the northern corner of the town, has that agreeable air of elegant fantasy only to be found in spots of this kind. Most of it dates from the early years of this century, when taking the cure was *de règle* throughout Europe.

51

Many visitors, past and present, came not to take the laxative and diuretic waters, but to observe the fashionable world. One of them was the great satirist Giuseppe Giusti, born at the nearby spa of Monsummano in 1809, whose poems were the scourge of Grand Duke Leopold's government and can still be relished today for their mordant, ruthless irony at the expense of tyranny and corruption.

A gentler side to Giusti's character made him deeply devoted to his native north Tuscan countryside, with its deep valleys, fast-flowing streams and hillsides clad in thick chestnut woods. It is said to have been Paolo Guinigi who encouraged chestnut planting, during his fifteenth-century ascendancy, to provide a source of flour for the mountain dwellers. Cooked in its traditional forms, such as the cake with rosemary and pine kernels known as *castagnaccio*, this stood their descendants in good stead during the hungry years of World War II. The stands of trees are at their thickest once you enter the Garfagnana, towards which the route now turns.

Retracing the road to Pescia, turn north through Collodi towards some fine examples of the region's best romanesque architecture. To the left, at Villa Basilica (once known as Villa Battiferri – 'wrought iron' – for its expert swordsmiths), there is a sturdy late thirteenth-century church, with an arcaded apse and crenellated campanile, and the bonus of a crucifix (*c.*1220) by Bonaventura Berlinghieri's Milanese father, Berlinghiero. Further west, take the dirt road across the hill to Brancoli, where the *pieve* of San Giorgio, among the most dignified romanesque incarnations, has carving of exceptional vigour in the sculpture around the font and at the bases of the pulpit columns.

From here, if still in search of variations on the *pieve romanica*, you will have to go a little south to cross the Serchio at Ponte a Moriano, and follow the right bank up to Diecimo. A little way out of the village, and easily

Right **West of Montecatini, the village of Buggiano Castello is one of the most attractive in the Lucchesia, with many houses covered in garishly-painted stucco, such as surrounds this doorway (*above*).**

spotted by its tall, white bell-tower, is the church of Santa Maria, one of the largest hereabouts, with some of those farouche pagan relief panels around the outer doorways which lend intrigue to the austerity of the style.

Thence, via Borgo a Mozzano, whose humpbacked medieval bridge was one of those said to have been built by the Devil in a single night, to a place suffused to an incredible degree with the sense of a vanished, irrecoverable moment in nineteenth-century social history. Bagni di Lucca, like the other Tuscan curative springs, was well known to early medieval Italy, when Countess Matilda or Frederick II chose to turn aside

Left The single-arched Ponte della Maddalena at Borgo a Mozzano was rumoured to have been built with the help of the Devil.

Houses at Bagni di Lucca overhang the romantic River Lima, where Shelley and Byron used to go boating.

from war and politics to bathe in its hot springs. Montaigne passed a delightful summer here in 1581, analysing the effects of the waters on his bowels in lurid detail, dancing with the peasantry, climbing the mountains and indulging that insatiable curiosity which provided the foundation for his essays. James Francis Edward Stuart, the Old Pretender, touched for the King's Evil in 1722 (the enraged British government threatened an embargo on Lucca olive oil) and five years later those two quintessentially eighteenth-century spirits Montesquieu and Lord Chesterfield visited the baths together, charming the company by their wit and sententiousness.

Who, indeed, was not at Bagni di Lucca? After the Napoleonic wars, it became a paradise for foreign expatriates, refugees from the sweltering Florentine summers with only a half-hearted interest in the water-cure itself. Here you might have watched Shelley and his friends preparing for that jolly picnic he describes in *The Boat on the Serchio*, Ibrahim Pasha, Viceroy of Egypt, strolling along the chestnut alleys with his exotically-garbed spahis, Flaubert arm-in-arm with Victor Hugo, and a crop of those minor novelists, Charles Lever, Francis Marion Crawford and Fanny Trollope, whose works formed the staple fare of English travellers abroad, and can still be enjoyed today by anyone with a good sense of the period.

Under the benign patronage of the harum-scarum Carlo Lodovico, Duke of Lucca, whose chief minister, Thomas Ward, had begun life as a Yorkshire jockey, there were horse-races in the dried-up river-bed and gambling at the casino. The Duke himself was, though charming, a thoroughly bad lot and had no hesitation, when things grew too hot for him financially and politically, in signing away his duchy to Tuscany in 1847 on the 'anything-for-a-quiet-life' principle. No wonder Robert Browning, according to his wife Elizabeth, had taken 'the strongest prejudice against these Baths of Lucca, taking them for a sort of wasps'

nest of scandal and gaming, and expecting to find everything trodden flat by the Continental English', though when the famous pair did arrive, in July 1849, they grew thoroughly enraptured with the beauty of the scene.

Nowadays there is something slightly shabby and depressing about it all. The stucco of the ornamental villas is peeling, the English church, in fantasy Tuscan gothic, is perpetually closed, the pretty neo-classical casino needs a lick of paint, and Prince Demidoff's domed rotunda chapel is fenced off with 'Danger' notices. Yet the cures go splendidly onwards, with steam grotto treatment for arthritis and obesity and mud baths for 'the pathology of the male reproductive organs'. The spa complex, in its attractive little courtyard at the top of the hill, is annually thronged with suffering enthusiasts.

Venus and Cupid, a neo-classical medallion at Bagni di Lucca.

Ghosts of former mud-bathers and vapour-inhalers haunt the Protestant cemetery beside the main Abetone road on the left bank of the Lima. To inspect the graves, go round to the back and climb over the wall: here, among the weeds and brambles, you will find a memorial to Ouida (Marie-Louise de la Ramée), that most scandalously popular of Victorian novelists, whose romances of smart society, like *Moths* and *Under Two Flags*, make rattling good reads, and the graves of the best and worst writers on Bagni di Lucca. Evangeline Whipple's *A Famous Corner of Tuscany* (1922) is as readable for the right reasons as Clotilda Elizabeth Stisted's *Highways and Byways of Italy* (1845) is enjoyable for the wrong ones.

Clotilda, however, was nothing if not 'A Character'. With her husband Henry, known to all as 'the dear old colonel', she presided over society at the baths, fawning on the Duke and his mother and playing the harp in a special costume designed to evoke spiritual thoughts. The dear old colonel himself played the 'cello, and when he died in Naples, his wife, in order to avoid paying the very heavy duties involved in transporting a dead body across four frontiers on the way home to Lucca, packed him and the 'cello into a huge box labelled 'second-hand goods, much damaged' and whisked him cheaply through the customs to his last resting-place here in the Protestant graveyard.

Turning westwards, you now enter the deeply incised upper valley of the Serchio, with its wooded mountain spurs, topped here and there with ruined towers and half-abandoned villages, the very stuff of romantic landscape enthusiasm. 'Their nobly rounded, lovely green forms', wrote the German poet Heinrich Heine in 1837, 'seem of themselves inspired by the civilization of art, and accord melodiously with the blue heaven.' Yes indeed, but the Garfagnana, as this region is called, was, in its human dimension, one of Tuscany's poorest and most disturbed areas, a counterpart to the southern Maremma in many

Castle and church seem to grow together at Ghivizzano near Barga.

respects. Lawlessness was rife until the middle of the nineteenth century, and subsequently the mountain towns became flourishing centres of anarchism. Mass emigration left many farms and hamlets derelict, and one modern Italian writer maintains (though I have not yet checked this) that many of England's original fish-and-chip shops had *garfagnini* proprietors.

Work could be found, however, in the paper-mills along the river bank, some of whose buildings, dating from the early nineteenth century, are among the oldest industrial architecture in Tuscany. Otherwise the peasantry made its living from chestnuts, stacked in special shelters known as *metati*, olives, whose oil is deemed the best in Italy, and whatever they could grow in their *chiusure*, hedged fields not found anywhere else in the province.

Keeping to the left bank, turn off at Fornaci di Barga up to Barga itself, sited most impressively on its hilltop within what remains of medieval ramparts and bastions. Tossed about between Lucca, Pisa and Florence, the town placed itself, in 1341, firmly under the protection of the Florentines, who encouraged its silk industry and the making of those plaster figurines which, as sold on trays by 'Italian image men', were a feature of Victorian London street life.

The slightly subdued attractions of Barga's steep, tortuous streets are enhanced each summer by an enterprising music festival, with performances of rarely heard operas in the little eighteenth-century Teatro dell' Accademia dei Differenti, in Piazza Angelio. Visitors are invariably drawn by the superbly-placed romanesque *duomo* of San Cristofano, perched on its grassy platform known as the Arringo (the English word harangue – literally 'to speak on a public platform' – derives from the same source).

This is a perfect small romanesque cathedral, with its ninth-century east end and successive stages added over the next three hundred years culminating in the exceptionally broad western façade, pierced by a single doorway with flanking lions on either side of the frieze. Restoration after an earthquake in 1920 was sensitively carried out. Under the sturdy square pillars of the short nave you can admire the carved masks on the twelfth-century water stoups in white and pink marble, the inlaid screens designed to divide male and female worshippers, and the exceptional pulpit, probably by Guido Bigarelli of Como, who flourished during the early thirteenth century. Every detail coheres in liveliness and strength, from the lions crushing sinners beneath their paws and the preying eagles on one of the capitals, to the sculptured panels of

Ancient lanes and alleys make up the centre of Barga, in the upper Garfagnana.

scenes from the life of Christ and the decorated black and white bands of stonework above and below them. And do not miss the colossal wooden statue of a glum-looking St Christopher, Christ Child on shoulder, behind the high altar, and the tenderly graceful canopied shrine by Luca della Robbia, with its elegant angels wearing somewhat unusual collars.

From Barga you can either take the road via Ponte di Catagnana to visit the house of the poet Giovanni Pascoli (1855–1912) at Castelvecchio, or rejoin the valley road. Both eventually carry you over the river and up into Castelnuovo di Garfagnana. This was a command post of the western spur of the Duchy of Modena, only becoming part of Tuscany in 1846 as a result of a deal between the two sovereign dukes, so that it is no surprise to find stone *stemme* (coats of arms) bearing the spread-winged eagle of the Este family, rulers of Ferrara and Modena. In the *rocca*, entered by grand turreted gateways, lived the great renaissance poet Ludovico Ariosto (1474–1533), whose work as governor of the Garfagnana was carried out largely so as to pay for a second edition of *Orlando Furioso*, that unforgettable poetic mishmash of allegory, myth, magic and romance.

How he loathed the job, the place and the people! He missed his wife and family, the 'rough, wild, horrid crags' frightened and depressed him, he was bored with the factious, quarrelsome populace, the constant disputes with Florence and Lucca, the intransigence and duplicity of his master Duke Alfonso of Ferrara and the way in which his efforts at reform were constantly thwarted. No wonder he wrote to the ducal secretary: 'I frankly confess that I am not a man to govern other men. I have too much pity and not enough courage to refuse what is asked of me.' His plea for recall was finally answered in June 1525, after three memorably ghastly years.

The road westwards from Castelnuovo takes you up into the Apuan Alps, the mountain range between here

TUSCANY

and the coast, whose height (1945 metres at the summit of Monte Pisanino) is the more impressive for the amazing suddenness with which the jagged peaks fling themselves skywards. This is one of the most dramatic highways in Tuscany, nearly fading out altogether amid the spectacular harshness of Monte Altissimo and Pian della Fioba, before zigzagging down past the little spa of San Carlo (water good for the liver and kidneys) and curving round towards Massa, with its views across the populous plain towards the sea.

Massa was once the capital of a tiny, independent state, ruled by the Cybo Malaspina family (one of the only Italian families to have the letter 'y' in its surname, for what such information is worth). They hung on to their lordship for over two centuries, from 1553 until 1790, but marriage with Modenese princes who had Hapsburg connections meant that the city could be readily handed over to Modena at the Congress of Vienna in 1815.

The Malaspina palace, in Via Alberica, is now a local government office, but you may get a glimpse of the pretty galleried baroque courtyard (1675–94) by Gian Francesco Bergamini. His son Alessandro was responsible for the façade, with its neat disposition of balconies and busts. Cross the Piazza Aranci and turn right down Via Dante, at the bottom of which you will find more Malaspina in the cathedral – most of them, in fact, lying in the family vault. The descent to this is through the chapel of the Holy Sacrament, with an opulent and expressive altarpiece by Alessandro Bergamini and a frescoed *Madonna* by Pinturicchio. Above the city, unmistakably dominant, is a fine medieval *rocca* which the Malaspina subsequently converted into a palace, at the same time strengthening and rebuilding the outer walls and bastions.

By acquiring Massa, the Dukes of Modena also got hold of the great marble quarries whose rich spoils created, and continue to create, the town of Carrara, a few kilometres to the north-west. Like Massa, Carrara has spilt down to the sea in an untidy semi-industrial sprawl, but it is worth threading your way through this to get a glimpse of so highly marmoreal a place. Marble stares at us from an array of singularly handsome façades, including that of the Accademia di Belle Arti, a former sixteenth-century Malaspina palace, in its eponymous piazza, the fourteenth-century house in Via Santa Maria where Petrarch is said to have stayed, and the Teatro degli Animosi, in Via Cesare Battisti. Built in 1840, this was much admired by Dickens, who heard the quarrymen sing a comic opera here and enjoyed it hugely.

At its most beautifully worked, marble adorns the cathedral of Sant'Andrea, which, rarely for this part of Tuscany, contrives a synthesis between romanesque and gothic. Work seems to have progressed slowly, from the eleventh century onwards, resulting in a gothic upper level featuring a gorgeous rose window set within delicately incised bands of decorative carving, and an apse with a row of ogival arches with sculptured heads, gently inclined, above the capitals. Within, it is the stonework, rather than the paintings, which demands notice: the sixteenth-century pulpit, the baroque saints, the early medieval high altar (1267–74) by Giroldo da Lugano are all witnesses to Carrara's gift to artists since Roman times.

Marble is crystallized limestone, metamorphosed by

Previous pages **San Terenzo, a coastal village near Lerici, on the borders of Tuscany and Liguria.**

Washing, green shutters and a dog, typical components of an Italian back street. This one is in Carrara.

intense heat. We are conditioned to think of it as an exclusively white substance, adorning the public buildings and cemeteries of northern Europe, but the variety of veined and variegated seams is immense, and to each of them Italian gives a resounding name, *bardiglio, paonazzo, cipollino, fior di pesco, arabescato, rosso di Castelpoggio, nero di Colonnata* and so on. You can visit a quarry by taking the road eastwards up to Colonnata itself, and watch, as Michelangelo himself watched, the cutting and preparation of the great blocks. In his day a wasteful technique of explosive blasting was introduced, only superseded in our own century by the use of drills and power-saws, cutting out some 700,000 tons of the stone per year.

Carrara used to be a stronghold – or, to use the charming Italian expression, *una santabarbara* (St Barbara being patroness of fortifications) – of the

This statue of Neptune at Carrara is supposed to represent the great Genoese admiral Andrea Doria.

Italian anarchist movement, but I doubt if there is much anarchist feeling left among *carraresi* suddenly enriched by a recent upturn in the marble trade. Money flows into the region from other sources besides. The whole of this coastline is one vast seaside resort, stretching right down from Marina di Carrara to Viareggio, so it is best to aim at minor roads via Seravezza and Pietrasanta on your way back to Lucca.

None of the seaside towns is particularly attractive, though their setting, on the narrow coastal plain known as the Versilia with the silvery screes and scarps of the Apuan Alps for a backdrop, is engaging enough. Only Viareggio itself genuinely deserves a visit, so brace yourself for crowded approach roads and spaghetti-junctions and plunge into the town.

Historic the place certainly is, from several aspects. It was, for a start, the very first sea-bathing resort in Italy, growing with the movement of the capricious Tyrrhenian shoreline around what had originally been the main seaport of the Republic of Lucca. Those two *vaches sacrées* Elisa Baciocchi and Duchess Maria Luisa were mainly responsible for turning it into a sedate and elegant summer retreat, favoured in later years by artists and writers (one of the nation's major literary prizes, the Premio di Viareggio, is awarded here each year). The Duchess decreed the separation of the sexes for bathing, with a fine of 7 lire for anyone crossing the boundary, and commissioned Lorenzo Nottolini in 1827 to lay out the grid plan Viareggio still retains, bounded at either end by sweeps of pine groves. Duke Carlo, characteristically, rescinded his mother's chaste ordinances and set up a casino besides.

Viareggio's heyday, however, came during the early years of the present century, in the boom years before the Great War, to which the term 'Italietta', meaning 'Little Italy', is contemptuously applied, and afterwards during the 1920s, when the actress Eleonora Duse, her playwright lover Gabriele d'Annunzio and their friends brought dash and cash to the place.

Puccini's statue surveys the gardens of his villa at Torre del Lago.

Italians rather loosely refer to the age's architectural style as 'liberty', basically anything from nouveau to deco; if you want an authentic flavour of it, go down to the sea front and walk along Viale Regina Margherita, where its super-kitsch inspirations blossom in florid abandon. Out of the moghul portals of the Gran Caffè Margherita, or under the sensuously curved windows of Magazzini Duilio or the embossed and carbuncled flim-flam of Bagno Balena (labelled 'an elegant coffin' at its opening in 1928), you might expect Pola Negri, Wanda Osiris, Isa Miranda or any other *femme fatale* of the entertainment world between the wars to come swanning to her impeccably-chauffeured automobile. And there is more of it in the boulevards beyond.

What the French call 'high vulgarization' lay at the heart of this entire culture, whose greatest artists were those who stood back from it. Giacomo Puccini (1858–1924) can be vulgar with the rest, but only the pompous and humourless would question his place among the deathless lyric dramatists. Like most Tuscans, the composer of *Bohème* and *Tosca* was loyal first and foremost to his native *terra*, where success, hard graft and an element of thoroughgoing but amiable ruthlessness in his character brought him his house by the lake of Massaciuccoli, at Torre del Lago on the southern edge of Viareggio. Most of his major works were composed here, between the hunting trips which were his other dominant passion (the cynical might add that a third was making women miserable). Guns and music are on display in the villa, where the composer and his crazily jealous wife are buried, and the lake itself, named after a Longobard farmer called Cuccolo, is a serene and unpolluted sheet of fresh water.

Viareggio sounds a sombre poetic echo as the scene of the famous cremation of the remains of Percy Bysshe Shelley on the beach during the afternoon of 16 August 1822. Sailing from Livorno to La Spezia in his yacht, the *Don Juan*, Shelley, with his friend Edward Ellerker Williams, was drowned, and his body, with a volume of Keats's poems in the pocket of his coat, was washed up a fortnight later at Gombo, south along the coast towards Pisa. It was Byron who, with the assistance of that shifty old yarn-spinner Edward Trelawny (indirectly responsible, some say, for Shelley's death, by encouraging him to have the yacht built too shallow) organized the last act. 'You can have no idea', he wrote to Thomas Moore, 'what an extraordinary effect such a funeral pile has, on a desolate shore, with mountains in the background and the sea before, and the singular appearance the salt and frankincense gave to the flame. All of Shelley was consumed, except his *heart*, which would not take the flame, and is now preserved in spirits of wine.

65

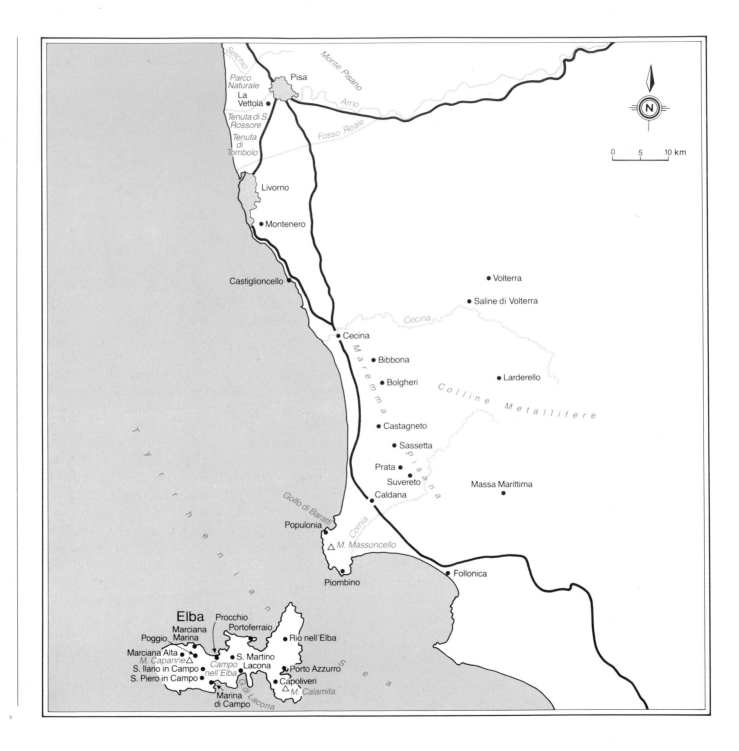

2
Pisa, Elba
and the Northern Maremma

Pisa – Livorno – Castiglioncello – Cecina –
Piombino – Portoferraio and Elba – Massa
Marittima – Larderello – Volterra

I have never cared for Pisa. Of all Tuscany's larger cities it is the one which least compels me either to linger or to return. Flung down on a plain beside the Arno, it makes few of those grand urban gestures we expect in Italy. None of its elements cohere: the 'temple complex' of the *duomo*, baptistery, leaning tower and Camposanto stands in chaste isolation, reached through the yellow town, grubby, squat and apologetic, with a stately Lungarno *alla fiorentina* tacked on mendaciously in the middle, and a dull workaday southern suburb, rebuilt after wartime bombing, towards the station.

Its history, largely a chronicle of vanity and greed, throws up little that is arresting or attractive in the way of characters and events. 'Better a corpse in the house than a Pisan at the door' say the Florentines, and the two cities have scant reason to love one another. Some of that mournful, reluctantly quiescent quality which clings to the city must always be owing to its subjection to Florence, the ultimate note of departed glory in Pisa's swift decline.

A charming tradition claims that Epeus, builder of the wooden horse of Troy, was washed ashore here with his fellow Greeks and that when their Trojan slaves burnt the ships, he founded a city named after an earlier Pisa in the Peloponnese. Certainly there was a Roman colony established here by 180 BC, a major harbour for refitting and victualling galleys, but the gradual silting of the river and the capricious fluctuations of the shoreline meant that by the beginning of the seventeenth century the city was wholly landlocked, the once redoubtable Porto Pisano had vanished, and the erstwhile maritime republic was simply a glorious memory.

In its heyday during the early Middle Ages, '*gloriosa Pisa*' was a major threat to the peace of the Islamic kingdoms dominating the western Mediterranean. Pisan ships harried the Moorish navies in Sardinia, Sicily and north Africa, and 120 vessels bore the Crusaders to the Holy Land in 1094, patriotic chroniclers claiming that two Pisans – Cucco Ricucchi and Coscetto di Colle – were the first to climb the walls of Jerusalem. For another two centuries the city's merchants could be found everywhere from the Balearic Islands to the Black Sea, with warehouses and wharves up and down the Crusader kingdoms and countries.

As a mercantile power Pisa flourished too early. Venice was starting to gain a crucial foothold in the commercial domains of the Levant, but Pisa's main rival was the hated Republic of Genoa. After nearly a hundred years of continual strife between the two cities, it was the Genoese who administered the *coup de grâce* to the already failing Pisan ascendancy at the decisive battle of Meloria in 1284, capturing or killing 16,000 men and seizing forty galleys. Ghibelline Pisa, surrounded by Guelph states such as Lucca and Florence, had little chance of political survival as an independent commune, and it was in 1406 that the Florentines took final possession of the town, worn out as it already was with endless internecine feuding between nobles and people.

It has never altogether recovered. The Medici, wise and considerate rulers as they invariably were, did their best to reawaken the city; the ancient university was re-established in 1574 with a fixed income, independent of monastic interference; the river and the canals were dredged and cleaned, and the grand-ducal court paid regular winter visits here. Yet the place has an eternal sombreness which not even the presence of what is generally considered Italy's finest university can entirely redeem.

Thus the focus of all pilgrimage to Pisa, that exceptional ensemble spread out across the vivid green meadow of the Campo dei Miracoli, has a vein of sadness running across its vibrant beauty. At the height of her potency and wealth, the republic began work, in 1064, on a great cathedral, to be faced entirely in variegated bands of marble, to the designs of the Pisan architect Buschetto, whose tomb is built into an arch to the left of the main porch. The immense basilica, with its four tiers of arcading on the western façade, Bonanno Pisano's magnificent bronze doors (1180) on the south-east entrance, with their elementally modelled scenes from the life of Christ, and

Pisa, like Florence, has its Lungarno, a splendid line of riverside palaces.

A view across the green lawns of the Campo dei Miracoli, Pisa.

its elliptical gothic dome by Lupo di Gante and Puccio di Gadduccio, provided a model and an inspiration for hundreds of other northern Italian churches: in a sense it can be seen as the ancestor of a tradition reaching down to the Baroque, and we catch the most unlikely echoes of its influence across the length and breadth of Europe.

The interior carries on this quality of elegant, wholly unselfconscious grandeur, taking up the mint-humbug striping of the outside in the patterns of the clerestory galleries – *matronei*, for female worshippers – running above the tall Corinthian columns of the nave. The vista through the crossing is closed in a great apsidal mosaic of *Christ between the Virgin and St John*, powerfully evocative of those countless images of 'Christos Pantokrator' to be seen in byzantine

churches. This is by the local painter Francesco di Simone di Porta a Mare, begun in 1301 and completed by no less a hand than Cimabue's a year later.

Much of the building is in fact a restored and re-ordered version of the original, put back together again after a disastrous fire in 1595. One of the casualties of the flames was the superb pulpit in the nave's north-east corner, only reassembled during the present century and now admired as the most outstanding creation of Giovanni Pisano, dating from 1302–10. Pisano is invariably ticketed with the 'Italian gothic' label, but this is only half the story: his use of acanthus-leaf scrolls and Corinthian capitals is as emphatically classicizing as the poses and drapery of the tall saints on either side of the intensely dramatic New Testament scenes running round the bowl of the pulpit, patently marked by the influence of Roman sarcophagi. Look out, incidentally, for Giovanni's beautiful ivory *Madonna*, in the Opera del Duomo museum next to the cathedral. This proud mother showing off her rather arrogant-looking Christ Child is much more blatantly gothic in its allusion to French models.

Of other treasures surviving the fire, the most notable must surely be Tino da Camaino's tomb of the Holy Roman Emperor Henry VII, originally placed in the Camposanto in 1315, two years after Henry's death, and now reconstructed in the south aisle. Henry, object of Ghibelline hopes and Dante's standard-bearer of Italian unity and order, died at Buonconvento near Siena, poisoned, it was said, with the Mass bread. The miserable Pisans, wrecking the town, seized the royal body and gave it a splendid funeral, sealing the grave of their hopes with Tino's magisterially carved effigy, above which is a niche with two frescoed angels by Ghirlandaio, painted a century later.

Every large romanesque church had its free-standing campanile, and on the cathedral's south-east

side stands the most famous of them all, symbolic not merely of Pisa, but of Tuscany and Italy besides. From its inception by Bonanno Pisano in August 1174, the leaning tower began to tilt and has become steadily more inclined over the following eight hundred years to the delight of travellers and the perturbation of the graver citizens of Pisa itself. 'The bending tower made so by exquisit art: as if to misse with art were a great mastery', recalled the English recusant Richard Lassels in 1654, supposing the tilt intentional. So did his

Pisa's leaning tower, where Galileo carried out his famous experiments, began to tilt when it was first built in 1174.

contemporary the diarist John Evelyn: 'the beholder would expect it to fall, being built exceedingly decliningly by a rare address of the architect; that and how it is supported from falling I think would puzzle a good geometrician.' At any rate this perpetual lurch enabled the greatest Pisan of them all, Galileo, to carry out his famous gravitational experiments on falling masses here, and tourists continue to enjoy scrambling up through the casing of marble arcades, the work of three other architects besides Bonanno, finished off in a sort of desperation by Tommaso da Pontedera in 1372, who clapped the bell-chamber on top with an even more pronounced sideways lean.

Along the other side of the cathedral runs the tall blank arcading of the Camposanto, the unique enclosed cemetery which has given a name and a form to every other throughout Italy. 'It's called the Campo Santo', Lassels tells us, 'because therein is conserved the Holy Earth brought from Hierusalem in fifty Gallies of this Republic . . . they returned home again laden with the earth of the Holy Land, of which they made this Campo Santo.' So indeed they did in 1188, but it took another ninety years before the massive cloister, with its rich fresco cycles by Benozzo Gozzoli and others, was finished. The sacred earth was accorded phenomenal properties of decomposition, and according to travellers it shrank the flesh off the bones in the space of 24 hours.

Alas, the heavy Allied bombing of Pisa in 1944 sent a river of molten lead from the roof running across the devastated walls and floors. The frescoes we see today, already seriously damaged by exposure to the salt breezes from the coast, are mere shadows of a former glory, though it is worth looking closely at the great *Triumph of Death* in its specially arranged gallery. Nobody knows the artist's name, though some like to suppose it was Andrea Orcagna or Ambrogio Lorenzetti, but the mixture of solemnity and in-tensely-focused observation here is chillingly impressive. Notice, for instance, the richly-garbed king, said to be a portrait of Uguccione della Faggiuola, whom Dante called the 'greyhound destined to save Italy', holding his nose as he gazes from his horse at the decomposing corpse of a fellow monarch, while the lady beside him looks on in distress.

The cloister of the Camposanto is littered with funerary sculpture of every period from the Hellenistic era to the Risorgimento, which offers a display the more absorbing for being unintentional. There are opulently sculpted Roman sarcophagi, several of which were recycled for medieval burials, and tombs such as those of the ill-fated Gherardesca family, chunks of Egyptian sculpture dug up at Thebes in 1828 by the Pisan archaeologist Ippolito Rossellini, and a number of those immensely dignified monumental

A lively romanesque detail from the arcades of the leaning tower, Pisa.

essays in neo-classicism by the Florentine carver Lorenzo Bartolini (1777–1850) and his followers. Am I alone in finding the mournful reserve and a certain quality of silence and suppression in such works extremely moving? I hope not.

The final component of what Dickens memorably termed 'the architectural essence of a rich old city, with all its common life and common habitations pressed out, filtered away' is arguably the most beautiful of all. This is the round baptistery, set well

Romanesque and gothic meet in the design of Pisa's baptistery.

73

apart from the *duomo*, and looking, with its successive layers of romanesque arcading and gothic pinnacles topped by a quaint, hat-shaped dome, like the ceremonial diadem of some king who died when 'there were giants in those days' and left his crown behind at Pisa. It was projected by the architect Deotisalvi (literally, 'God save you'), who left his name – 'Deotisalvi Magister Hujus Operis' – on the column to the left of the door, but died before he could complete the work.

Inside, marble banding on the walls reflects the pattern in the cathedral, and here is a yet nobler pulpit, the work of Giovanni Pisano's father Nicola (1220–78), dated 1260 and an evident model in most respects for its more ornate counterpart. The classical touches here are less learned and more solid: clumps of Corinthian columns divide scenes in which the figure of the Virgin is patently offered to us as a Roman matron, and the squirming bodies of the *Last Judgment* represent a pioneer assault on the challenge of nude forms. Before leaving the baptistery, try the ringing echo under the dome.

From the Campo dei Miracoli, follow Via Capponi past the archbishop's palace and into Via dei Martiri, which leads you towards the only really attractive square in the city. The Piazza dci Cavalieri is said to occupy the site of the Roman forum, which later became the medieval Piazza delle Sette Vie. On the north side, to the left of the arch under the clock, the walls of the seventeenth-century Palazzo dell'Orologio incorporate the remains of the notorious Torre Gualandi, among the most famous towers in world literature. In 1287 Count Ugolino della Gherardesca, Pisa's leading Guelph, whose faineant conduct against the Genoese at Meloria had already excited suspicion of treachery, was seized in a Ghibelline coup and imprisoned here, with two sons and two grandsons. Food was forbidden to all five captives, who shortly died of hunger. The Count's pleas for absolution had been ignored and the corpses were given the humblest of funerals, but though the Pisans were universally execrated, Archbishop Ruggieri, who had awarded the fatal sentence, ignored the Pope's angry interdict. As portrayed by Dante in Canto XXII of the *Inferno*, Ugolino and his family captured the romantic imagination some five centuries later: Blake, Reynolds and Fuseli painted them, and Donizetti set the entire passage to music as a declamatory cantata.

To the right of Palazzo dell'Orologio is the immense Palazzo dei Cavalieri, a Vasarian remodelling of a medieval palace, whose present appearance, together with the church of Santo Stefano next door, is more Roman than Tuscan. The grey and white *sgraffito* decoration scratched on the façade may not be universally appealing, but the busts of the grand dukes peeping from their niches, ugly mugs as only the Medici could have, add a welcome human touch to an essentially dull building.

The palace used to be called the Carovana, from the Persian word meaning 'journey' or 'company'. This name reflected the special training course of the Knights of Santo Stefano, who spent four years here learning the art of war against the Turks, for which Cosimo I founded the Order in 1562. Captured Ottoman trophies hang in the church, begun by Vasari and finished in 1594 by Bernardo Buontalenti. The unorthodox design with an open hall reached through doors from the side aisles is due to a seventeenth-century conversion of the original plan. Look up at Alessandro Pieroni's richly carved ceiling, a flamboyant frame to pictures of stirring moments in the early years of the Order by Cigoli, Ligozzi and

The Palazzo Gambacorti was built for a Pisan nobleman at the end of the fourteenth century.

Cristofano Allori. The high altar is a masterly essay in baroque, with saints from the hand of Giovanni Battista Foggini, a sculptor whose stylish, energetic lines place him firmly in the best traditions of Tuscan carving.

Via San Frediano takes you out of the lopsided square and past the main university buildings to the Lungarno Pacinotti, from which there is as good a prospect as any of Pisa's successful attempt to repeat the Florentine effect in handsome sweeps of marble-clad palaces along the riverside, each with its neat compliment of green or brown shutters. If you turn to the left, along the Lungarno Mediceo, you will eventually reach Palazzo Toscanelli, formerly known as Palazzo Lanfranchi. From 1821 to 1822 this was the home of Lord Byron, driven from Ravenna under a cloud of suspicion for his support of the revolutionary Carbonari. Shelley and his harem of adoring women-folk were already in residence on the opposite side of the river in one of the so-called Tre Palazzi, once the property of the Corsini family. Shelley adored Pisa, and what was to be the last year of his life was enhanced by new friendships, notably with Trelawny, who wrote the most moving account of his death, and Edward Ellerker Williams, his companion on the ill-fated maiden voyage of the *Don Juan*. Williams's wife Jane provided one of those *amitiés amoureuses* Shelley apparently could not do without, as did the Contessina Emilia Viviani, the Pisan muse of *Epipsychidion*.

As for Byron, with his five carriages, nine saddle horses, dogs and cats, he was an object of continued suspicion to the Tuscan police, who thought all the English colony, which included the poets Leigh Hunt and Walter Savage Landor, dangerously mad. If they needed confirmation of this opinion, it came when the poet and his servants were involved in a brawl with some dragoons, an incident which sent the expatriates rallying to Palazzo Lanfranchi in defence of their literary lion. 'I thought, had he been an Italian', wrote the novelist Guerrazzi, then a student at Pisa, 'his compatriots would have assembled to stone him, and I began to understand why the English are a great people, and the Italians a bundle of rags in the shop of a second-hand dealer.'

Round the corner from Shelley's palace is the birthplace, in the Via della Fortezza, of Galileo Galilei, born on 18 February 1564, only two months before Shakespeare and, like him, one of the great shaping liberators of the enquiring imagination. If you want to see the books and instruments of the man himself, however, you should cross the river to the Domus Galileana in the Via Santa Maria. Should you do so, return to strike westwards along the Lungarno to see the last of Pisa's major treasures, the miniature gothic church of Santa Maria della Spina.

Reconstructed in the nineteenth century so as to save it from flood damage, it formerly stood almost on the water itself, its crockets, merlons and finials making it appear like some fantastic marine beast risen from the depths to dry its hard white scales in the sun. The Gualandi family built it in 1323 to shelter a thorn (*spina*) from Christ's crown, and the figures of saints above the windows are the work of pupils and siblings of Giovanni Pisano. As the church is practically never open, it is likely you will have to content yourself with admiring the singular sophistication of its gothic language, so markedly French in accent.

What Henry James calls 'Pisa's morbid charm' soon starts to pall, and I like to hurry out in search of a less claustrophobic atmosphere beyond the city limits. To the east on the slopes of Monte Pisano, the ancient frontier with Lucca, lies the splendid Charterhouse of Calci, one of the most invigorating baroque buildings in the region. Though the Cistercians originally settled here in 1366, nearly all of what survives, cloisters, chapels and the church itself, belongs to the seventeenth and eighteenth centuries. Something about the yellow and white west front of the monastery, with its curved pediments framing a pair of clocks, the elegance of the central façade and the double staircase rising to meet it, suggests another country altogether, Bavaria maybe, or Portugal, hinting at a certain sensuous frivolity wholly alien to Tuscan *serietà*. This joyous spirit is cheerfully carried over into the particoloured marbles of the church and into a riot of unremarkable frescoes, more handsome than holy, but surely none the worse for that in their context.

West of Pisa, surrounding routes to the sea, is the Tenuta di San Rossore, one of the oldest parks in Italy, a colossal stretch of pine forest running practically all the way from Viareggio as far south as Livorno. Browsed by deer, wild boar and goats, it was also roamed, until recently, by the descendants of the herd of dromedaries begun by Grand Duke Ferdinand II in 1622 and established as a going concern by his successor Francis II in the eighteenth century. The camels numbered 150 or so until World War II. Used for carrying heavy loads of wood, they always looked more Oriental than African in their general shagginess, a trait owed to interbreeding with animals captured from the Turks.

The coastline hereabouts is in a perpetual state of flux, exacerbated nowadays by innumerable building and engineering works both on land and on water. If you take the minor road towards Livorno via La Vettola, you soon arrive at the amply-proportioned romanesque basilica of San Pietro a Grado, which once dominated the now utterly vanished Porto Pisano, where the galleys of the maritime republic unloaded their freights of silk, spices, marble columns or returning pilgrims. This is the very spot where St Peter is said to have first set foot in Italy, and over his altar, close to the landing steps by the Arno, *ad gradus arnensis*, he commanded a church to be built.

Implausible as the story seems (what, one might ask, were the local governor's reactions?), fragments of Roman masonry are incorporated into the walls of the triple-apsed church, raised during the mid twelfth century, and excavations in the nave floor have disclosed early Christian foundations. Above the arches runs a not especially distinguished fresco sequence by the Lucchese artist Deodato Orlandi, painted around 1300, with a central band of scenes from the life of St Peter framed by papal portraits below and angels at open windows above.

Railway enthusiasts may wish to perform an act of piety by taking the train from Pisa to Livorno. This was only the second commercial track in Italy, begun in 1841 under the direction of George Stephenson's son Robert, and completed three years afterwards. In the presence of the Grand Duke and Duchess, the first train was solemnly blessed by the archbishop of Pisa, careless, it would seem, of the wrath of his master the Pope, who had denounced steam power as the work of the devil. 'To the playing of the band', says a report in the *Gazzetta di Firenze*, 'the signal for departure was given. The steam trembled to break free from the tubes of the machine. Columns of dense smoke arose, the whistle warned the guards to close the gates onto the line, and amid the applause of an immense crowd scattered across the adjacent fields, the first loco-motive to be seen among us set off on its journey.' A journey of 17 minutes, incidentally: it is not much less today.

Livorno – though I prefer to use the old English name 'Leghorn' – is lively enough by dint of being one of Italy's major seaports, but most of whatever visual attractiveness it may have possessed was wiped out by an annihilating German bombardment in 1943. The whole city, in whatever guise, is a monument to Medicean intelligence and enterprise. It was Cosimo I and his son Ferdinand who created, almost from nothing, a great free port, through which the wealth and commercial acumen of all nations, regardless of race or religion, was to flow with the inevitable object

77

Livorno's massive harbour bastions bear witness to the Medici's determination to turn it into a great seaport.

of enriching Tuscany. There were Huguenots and Flemings, fugitive Moors from Spain, a notable English community with its own 'factory', and one of the most active and energetic of Italian Jewish populations, protected by a special charter called *La Livornina*. For three hundred years this was one of those blessed Mediterranean towns which flourished until the cancer of nationalism undermined their essentially cosmopolitan flavour. Smyrna, Beirut and Alexandria are typical casualties, but Livorno, with its docks, its naval academy, its fishmarkets and canal basins, has somehow managed to hang on to its essence.

Once its exports included boracic acid, briar root, hemp, coral, marble, pumice stone, orris root and the straw bonnets, made at Signa near Florence, much in favour with English girls at the turn of the century. Among its imports were slaves, whose number, noted Evelyn in 1644, 'is prodigious; some buying, others selling, others drinking, others playing, some working, others sleeping, fighting, singing, weeping, all nearly naked and miserably chained.' Four of these, the Quattro Mori, surround the statue of Ferdinand I in Piazza Giuseppe Micheli, overlooking the old dock basin. The figure of the duke, in his costume of Grand Master of the Order of Santo Stefano, is by Giovanni Bandini, and the bronze Moors are from the gifted

Pietro Tacca's fettered Moors are reminders that Livorno was once an important slave market.

hand of Pietro Tacca (1577–1640). Above them hangs the Fortezza Vecchia, whose foundations date from the days of Countess Matilda.

The other 'lions' of Livorno are not many, but worth tramping the city to view. South along the waterfront into Piazza Mazzini takes you to Via Giuseppe Verdi where, half-way down, is the overgrown English cemetery, closed in 1839. Among the tumbled marbles is the memorial column marking the grave of Tobias Smollett, who died here in 1773, having combined a medical career with that of a justly popular novelist, who also managed to write a wondrously combative account of his Italian travels. North of the burial ground, in Viale Carducci, an extraordinary Doric portico, in the height of musclebound neo-classic taste, with an immense niche above it, marks the entrance to the municipal reservoir. This is the Cisternone, completed in 1842 by the great Pasquale Poccianti (1774–1858), whose career as state architect spanned the reigns of three grand dukes.

Lastly, if you feel energetic enough, go down to the Villa Fabbricotti, on the city's southern edge, where the civic museum holds a collection of paintings by the late nineteenth-century Tuscan group known as the *macchiaioli*, literally 'spot-makers', owing to their discreetly impressionist technique. I can never honestly muster much enthusiasm for their manner, leaden and uninspired as it so often appears, but many others beyond his native Livorno praise Giovanni Fattori (1825–1908), whose canvases dominate the gallery.

A more accessible painterly talent was that of Amadeo Modigliani, born to a Jewish family here in 1884. He spent the last fourteen years of his short life in Paris, spurning the blinkered provincialism of the *livornesi*. His attitude echoed that of Grand Duke Pietro Leopoldo, whose withering denunciation of the city and its inhabitants at the close of the eighteenth century accuses them of 'disharmony, malignity,

The nineteenth-century patriot Domenico Guerrazzi in his prison cell, Livorno.

facetiousness and scandalmongering; without religion or morals, they are devoted solely to the pursuit of commerce, a merchant class of liars and libertines, with ignorant priests and a still more ignorant populace, superstitious, fanatical, thieving and only kept in check by excessive rigour'.

Smollett might have agreed, but he passed his last year in Italy enjoyably enough by writing the immortal *Humphry Clinker* at Montenero, just off the main coast road to the south. The hilltop sanctuary here is one of those ancient shrines of the Mother Goddess converted to Christian uses scattered the length and breadth of Italy: its wonder-working icon of the Madonna and Child is supposed to have floated all the way from Negropont (Euboea in Greece). This icon used to be stamped on the bill of health for any

ship entering Livorno harbour as a tribute to the fact that a vessel suspected of plague had been refused entry and carried the epidemic to Marseilles instead.

The road south through the Maremma Pisana contains, as the old guidebook writers always say, 'little to detain the traveller'. Except, that is, for beach upon beach of coarse volcanic sand and resorts still small enough and spaced sufficiently far apart to be tolerable. You should try, wherever possible, to avoid the main Via Aurelia, crowded and dangerous in the tourist season, and turn off instead towards the little hill villages such as Bibbona, Bolgheri and Castagneto. Bibbona has a splendid prospect across the plain to the sea, where the beach, even at high season, is seldom very busy and, in the stretch beyond the statutory clutch of holiday villas and camp sites, totally deserted. Bolgheri, with its curious octagonal baroque chapel of San Guido at the lower crossroads, is approached through a long cypress avenue, celebrated in an ode by Giosué Carducci (1835–1907), a poet more honoured than read nowadays, but still considered one of nineteenth-century Italy's great lyric voices.

Davanti a San Guido is a humorous and touching *mélange* of childhood memories and meditations on literary fame. You can reach Castagneto, where Carducci spent his not terribly happy youth, by a pleasant drive along the edge of the hills south of Bolgheri. In the old fortified town his eccentric father tormented the boy with an education on the dubious 'cruel-to-be-kind' principle, killing his pet falcon and sending away the owl and the wolf which country-loving Giosué had tamed and befriended; but memory softened everything for Carducci, and the Maremma became, for the adult poet, a landscape of nostalgic enchantment.

From here it is worth taking the extremely circuitous but invariably attractive road via Sassetta and Prata over the high ridges to Suvereto on its little lookout hill, and then turning south-west to the sea

again. Crossing the Aurelia and the railway at Caldana, veer left on to the Piombino road, and take the right turn to Populonia. This is the old Etruscan Pupluna, where the copper from mines in the hinterland and the iron ore from Elba was smelted for export. The place languished after its destruction by Sulla in 79 BC, but you can still see the Etruscan chamber tombs in their mounds like rum-baba moulds on the green plain by the seashore, and a small museum in the town contains finds from local excavations.

Pine trees are a typical feature of Tuscany's coastal landscape. This avenue is near Piombino.

81

The gulf of Baratti, which Populonia commands, is enjoyably free of mass tourism; the beaches are sandy and the bathing excellent. Between here and Piombino Monte Massoncello sticks out into the Tyrrhenian Sea like a breakwater. Alas, whatever charms Piombino may once have possessed are nowadays overwhelmed by heavy industry; after it had passed through a long line of princely Roman owners, Napoleon gave it to his sister Elisa Baciocchi, but the woman who made such an indelible mark on northern Tuscany left no worthwhile traces here.

Matters Napoleonic should nevertheless dominate your thoughts at this point, for Piombino is the ferry port for the island of Elba, where the Emperor spent nine months in exile, from May 1814 to February 1815, before escaping to France, to the brief return to power known as the Hundred Days, Waterloo, and the culminating indignity of Saint-Helena. The naïvety of the victorious allies in sending him to the island passes belief. Arrogant, pompous and domineering as always, he started rapping out imperial orders as soon as he arrived, while maintaining a secret correspondence with mainland Italy, not particularly ecstatic at being reduced to a second-rate province of the Hapsburg empire and longing for a return to Bonapartism.

Within a few days the entire island economy had been shaken up. The inhabitants were told to dig proper drains, plant more chestnuts and olives, grow potatoes and make proper roads. In between drafting minutes for such enterprises, Napoleon set up an immense court establishment and an army which included the cadets of a military academy and the newly-arrived veterans of the Imperial Guard, led by Marshal Cambronne whose famous 'Merde!' at Waterloo has passed into legend. Moving restlessly around Elba with his train of 27 carriages, the Emperor spent much of his time setting up palaces for himself, to be paid for by severe taxes on the Elbans. The Italians' remarkable unwillingness to bear collective

grudges, however, meant that when his nephew Napoleon III lost his throne in the Franco-Prussian war half a century later, the islanders were ready to invite him to spend his exile among them. The offer, however, was tactfully declined in favour of a gloomy house on the road between Sidcup and Chislehurst in England.

Agreeable *causeries* with his favourite sister Pauline Borghese and a brief visit from his devoted Polish mistress Marie Walewska formed a prelude to the real business in hand, Napoleon's flight to France, which took the form of a very public embarkation during the unaccountably prolonged absence of the English Commissioner, Sir Neil Campbell, in Livorno. No longer a miniature empire, Elba was returned to the Grand Duchy of Tuscany and to the footnotes of history.

Portoferraio, the island's capital, appears at its most impressive from the sea, clenched as it is in the grip of a pair of Medicean forts built by Cosimo I in 1548 as part of a scheme to develop the harbour under the grandiose title of Cosmopoli. The chosen architect was Giambattista Camerino, whose boast was that the two forts, Stella and Falcone, were constructed in such a way that neither might fire on the other in the event of enemy capture. This was ironical, since Camerino himself was later to be killed by a musket shot while directing an artillery exercise at a castle in the Chianti. Benvenuto Cellini's bronze bust of Cosimo, formerly above the gate of Forte della Stella, is now in the Bargello at Florence.

The old town, as distinct from the modern harbour with its metal foundries, retains its Mediterranean seaport character, with stepped streets up the hillside under jolly festoons of laundry. It is worth toiling up

---

Safe from raiding corsairs, Poggio lies high up on Elba's central hills.

Left Elba's island coastline is a series of promontories and heavily indented bays.

Above Minerva, significantly unarmed, surveys Napoleon's garden on Elba.

to the piazza between the two forts which contains the Villa dei Mulini, Napoleon's palace, which the Emperor cleverly knocked together from a brace of windmills. The internal effect is a sort of Malmaison in little, with gilt Empire chairs, the great man's bed, his library (a heterogeneous collection including several volumes of fairy-tales, books on dyeing cotton and making brandy, and the novels of Fanny Burney) and a large room to one side of the house where Pauline and the courtiers got up amateur theatricals. But it is in the garden, looking across the strait towards Piombino, that the presence of this restless little man, who had overturned the world for more than a decade, becomes irresistible, and we almost expect to see him conning the hazy Tuscan shore with his telescope.

From Portoferraio a road westwards leads up to his country house, the Villa San Martino, containing more *bonaparteries* amid some engaging neo-classical fresco work by Pietro Ravelli. It is difficult to know why Anatol Demidoff, husband of the Emperor's niece Princess Mathilde, wanted to build the singularly unappealing one-storey palace on the slope below. Intended as a memorial, it was opened in 1851 but shut very soon afterwards in a fit of lordly pique due to some fancied slight on the islanders' part, and now houses a gallery with several good examples of Italian nineteenth-century portraiture, a field only recently getting its due from critics and historians.

Enough of the Corsican ogre. Elba's beauty, that softened, undramatic charm of the western Mediterranean, needs no such recommendations to explore it. The various ends of the island, which is shaped rather like one of those protoplasmic organisms drawn in school biology lessons, each possess a marked individuality, owing to a mixed and complex geology. If, for example, you take the easterly road out of Portoferraio, you cross a high limestone ridge containing the iron ore for which Elba has been mined since Roman times (the capital began as Fabricia –

'factory' – and became Portoferraio – 'port of the iron workers'). The dirt track, as it soon becomes, crosses the typical *macchia* countryside of cistus, agave and prickly pear, with wonderful seascapes beyond and the grizzled old Pisan ruin called the Volterraio on its rocky crest, before teetering down at the crossroads, either to the village of Rio nell'Elba or towards the postcard *bijou* of Porto Azzurro, surrounding its little bay.

Beyond Porto Azzurro the southern peninsula of Capoliveri, dominated by the magnetic hill of Monte Calamita (the name means 'lodestone'), is still one of the less populous corners of Elba, though a rash of holiday villas litters the slopes above Morcone beach. Capoliveri itself, high up amid vineyards producing sweet *moscato* wine, was once a sort of open prison for medieval Pisan debtors, but has lost whatever grimness of aspect it may once have held and is nowadays famous for its fish stew called *sburrida*. From here you can look out westwards across the system of gulfs and promontories which makes up the southern coastline.

The western end of Elba is dominated by the great granite massif of Monte Capanne, scattered with vineyards and chestnut woods stretching down to the clifftop road. Unlike the northern coast around Portoferraio or the gulf of Lacona in the south, there is practically no good bathing here, and dusty mountain walkers will have to wait until Marciana Marina in its rocky bay. The little port was an offshoot of the much older Marciana Alta, always said to be the island's first inhabited spot, huddled up defensively against the mountainside. Uncannily, it still retains the sense of refuge and alertness that was imprinted on it as a place of safety from raiding Genoese, Spaniards or the

Rio nell'Elba, in the heart of the island's ancient mining district.

Left **A distant prospect of Marciana Marina, Elba.**

Above **Lemon trees bloom in a quiet corner of Marciana Marina.**

Barbary corsairs who periodically sacked the villages and carried off the Elbans into slavery.

The almost hysterically tortuous road eastwards past the ruined romanesque *pieve* of San Giovanni takes you down into the area known as Campo, with its olives and vines, and the comparably attractive villages of Sant'Ilario and San Piero. The latter has fragments of fifteenth-century fresco in the parish church, raised over a Roman temple to the minor deity Glaucus, patron of shipwrecked sailors, and a romantically ruined fortress. If you are unable to choose between heading north towards Procchio or south to Marina di Campo, I would emphatically take the Procchio direction, since, though Elba is never intolerably tourist-cluttered even at the height of the

Tuscan neo-classicism in a church porch at Follonica.

season, Marina is the most obvious seaside resort on the island, with all the attendant disadvantages.

Returning to the mainland, take the road from Piombino due east towards Massa Marittima, the only real visual reward among the large towns of south-west Tuscany and of crucial significance in the Maremma's mournful history. Despite what the guidebooks tell you, it never stood on the sea, but took its name from being the dominant city of this part of the coastal region, deriving its wealth from the mines of the Colline Metallifere to the north. A free commune from 1225 onwards, Massa hedged its bets between Pisa and Siena, but it was the Sienese who conquered in the end. After the Grand Duke gained control in 1555, the town began its slow decline, halted only by the Maremma's gradual recall to life in the nineteenth century.

Like other places in Italy, Massa is really two settlements, the lower Città Vecchia, gathered around the *duomo*, and the Città Nuova up the hill in the shadow of the Sienese fortress, and it is worth noting a preponderance of romanesque in the one and gothic in the other. The two were sometimes at war with one another, as the turbulent nobles of the *contado* turned their handsome palaces into strongholds and espoused rival causes.

The essence of this medieval combination of toughness and grace is distilled by the ensemble of the Piazza Garibaldi, the perfect statement, you may feel, of the piazza principle, at the heart of the Città Vecchia. Mounted, or rather exhibited, on its surrounding flights of steps, the cathedral of San Cerbone is the ultimate expression of mature Pisan romanesque, its blind arcading resistlessly urging the eye, via the gentle slope of the aisle roofs, towards the loggia and

Right **Massa Marittima, clustered in the shadow of a Sienese fortress.**

crockets above. St Cerbonius himself, who narrowly escaped martyrdom at the hands of the savage Ostrogoth Totila, who ordered him to be thrown to the bears, figures in the carved reliefs over the central porch. He appears again in the decoration of his marble sarcophagus in the crypt, the work of the Sienese sculptor Goro di Gregorio (note the bears licking the saint's feet and the depiction of the miracle in which Cerbonius milks does to provide drink for the Pope's thirsty servants). The painted panel of the *Madonna delle Grazie* in the north transept is obviously by an artist who had looked closely at the work of Duccio – Simone Martini maybe, but then again maybe not.

It is worth walking round the back of the gold-coloured church, with its campanile whose windows grow in number as the tower gets higher, to see in what an elegant gothic idiom it was eventually completed. Massa's brief moment of civic confidence is mirrored in the Palazzo Pretorio, opposite the *duomo*, built in 1230 and stuck with the customary coats of arms, including the Sienese she-wolf. From the mullioned window on the right, the *podestà* (mayor) Nicoluccio Mignanelli was flung to his death during a riot in 1318. Beside the palace are the restored Loggia del Comune, the bishop's palace and the medieval mint, the Palazzina della Zecca, where the city issued its own coinage. These were its great days, before Siena and the Maremma nearly killed it between them: by 1737 the population was reduced to just 500, the local proverb went '*Vai a Massa, guardala e passa*' – 'Go to Massa, look and pass on' – and only the sterling efforts of the Lorraine Grand Dukes rescued it at all.

At the western end of the square, the tall, crenellated Palazzo Comunale holds the municipal

---

A romanesque *duomo* and a renaissance palace in the heart of Massa Marittima.

picture gallery, whose chief glory is the *Madonna and Child enthroned among Saints*, an opulently conceived triptych in the most exalted early Sienese manner, the work of Ambrogio Lorenzetti who painted it around 1330. On the steps at the Virgin's feet sit Faith, Hope and Charity. Faith, dressed in green, contemplates a double-faced image of the Old and New Testaments in a mirror; Hope, wearing blue, carries a tower surmounted by a floating jewelled crown; and red-robed Charity bears the flaming heart and barbed arrow of love, while musical angels and others wafting incense wreathe the company in sensual harmonies.

The road north takes you into the heart of the Colline Metallifere, where part of Tuscany's own early nineteenth-century industrial revolution took place. During the 1840s the French mining engineer François de Larderel was able to harness the natural boracic geysers puffing from the ground hereabouts to a device for extracting boric acid. The result was Larderello, a name conferred by Leopold II, one of Italy's first industrial settlements, complete with model dwellings for the workers, schools, a hospital, a theatre and an academy of draftsmanship. Amid the plume-like fumaroles and the smoke from the cooling towers, this all comes as something of a shock after the sublimities of Lorenzetti, but it is just as valid a part of Tuscany's history, and incongruity is in any case a good cure for travellers' complacency.

Apprehensions thus sharpened, you reach the frowzy little mining village of Saline di Volterra, when the road begins its slow ascent, in positively intestinal loops, towards Volterra itself. I hesitate to recommend you to look over your shoulder during this climb, but the view across the bald yellow Maremma hills to the sea is one of those which clutches at the heart and makes you never want to abandon Italy. Volterra is in any case among the holy places of Tuscan journeying, possessed of that slightly withdrawn, hermetic loveliness which all the old Etruscan cities have retained as a proof of their wisdom in chucking away worldly supremacy or commercial success.

Ancient Velathri, the 'lordly Volaterrae' of Macaulay's 'How Horatius kept the Bridge', became a flourishing Roman town (the satirist Persius was born here) and spent much of the early Middle Ages in a tussle with overweening Florence, which wanted a firm hold on its valuable alum mines. In 1472 Lorenzo de' Medici and Federico da Montefeltro, Duke of Urbino, drew up their forces before the city, which, after a two months' siege, they sacked and pillaged with a ferocity unprecedented even in those days. Guilt at breaking his word of honour to the citizens clung to Lorenzo until his last moments, when he is said to have numbered it among the three principal sins he confessed to Savonarola on his deathbed.

The town is spread out across a long plateau within its medieval girdle of walls, but the remains of the Etruscan rampart, stretching to the edge of the dramatic landslip known as Le Balze, suggest that its earliest extent was much larger. The most impressive Etruscan survival is the Porta all'Arco, whose cyclopean masonry is crowned with an arch bearing three sandstone heads, supposedly lions, though nobody seems quite certain.

This is on the south wall, but the road from Massa actually brings you in at the western end of the town, and you would do well to get out at the car-park and explore the narrow streets on foot. There is nothing seriously ugly in Volterra, and only by walking here and there can you properly enjoy those small details – doorways, fragments of stonework, sculptured car-touches and shields, the shapes of arch and balcony – which give any Tuscan city its memorable sharpness of identity. At the end of Via San Lino, climb the steep Via Franceschini, from which you enter Piazza San Giovanni, the cathedral square.

I cannot explain why I like the unevenness and angularity of this open space so much, except by comparing it with its more orthodox counterparts elsewhere in Italy. It is nearly always quite empty, but the canted, bevelled planes of the *duomo*, baptistery and surrounding *palazzi* give the impression that invisible hands will change everything round to take up utterly different stations when you come back an hour or so later from lunching off the local wild boar, or the Volterran dish of pasta cooked with garlic, rosemary and tomato known as *minestra sullo scio* – 'slippery soup'.

As for the cathedral, its simplicity disarms criticism. This is the best sort of Italian church, in which decorative elements are flung together hugger-mugger so that good taste never anaesthetizes the possibilities for astonishment. Look up at the nave roof, for instance, with its perpetually watchful saints, carved in monstrous foreshortened relief by Iacopo Paolini and Francesco Cipriani in 1584. Look at Mino da Fiesole's white marble ciborium, with its sequence of kneeling angels, or at the bands of inlaid marble on the romanesque pulpit framing sculpture by a provincial follower of the Pisano family, or at the oddly moving awkwardness of the lanky figures in the painted wooden *Deposition* in the south transept. And do not ignore Sansovino's font in the octagonal gothic baptistery of 1283, whose dome and marble stripes make it thoroughly oriental in appearance.

From here turn down Via Turazza into the Piazza dei Priori, the kind of architectural ensemble calculated to induce that frisson of pleasure which hardened Italophiles experience when they realize that nowhere else on earth could possibly hold this sort of austere beauty. On the south-east corner is the Palazzo dei Priori, oldest of its kind in Tuscany, begun in 1208 to designs by Riccardo da Como, whose name is over the portal. Get up the tower if you can, and look out over the crumpled brown blanket of the Maremma, blotched with the drifting shadow of the clouds. The Palazzo Pretorio opposite is restored thirteenth-century work, the southernmost of whose two towers is always called the *Porcellino*, from the jolly little piglet rampant on its plinth at the top. Even the mock-medieval savings bank next to this scarcely looks out of place beside the fifteenth-century bishop's palace over the former loggia of the grain market.

Now you can either go under the arch into Via Buonparenti or, if it is evening, join the *volterrani* in their *passeggiata* down Via Matteotti, past the bars selling wild boar sandwiches and the confectioners displaying biscuits called, with macabre fitness, *ossa di morte* – 'bones of the dead'. Either way will bring you into Via Sarti, at the end of which stands Palazzo Minucci-Solaini, a tall fifteenth-century house which must surely be the work of the elder Antonio da San Gallo (1455–1534). This has very recently been converted to house the municipal picture gallery, one of the more rewarding in this part of Tuscany if only because Volterra chose its painters so discerningly.

Ghirlandaio arrests us here with his *Christ in Glory* above the Volterran martyrs Attinea and Greciniana (note the hawk-nosed profile of the Camaldolese abbot Giusto Bonvicini in the lower right-hand corner). Signorelli's *Annunciation* is elegant and mysterious as ever, and there is a luminous *Deposition* by the Flemish Mannerist Pieter de Witte (1540–1628) and a *Madonna in Glory* by the seventeenth-century local hand of Baldassare Franceschini, 'Il Volterrano' (1611–89), in which the sentimentalized Virgin is less striking than the unshakeably noble figures of surrounding saints. There is even a work or two by the notorious Daniele da Volterra, whose chief claim to fame is his commission from prudish Paul V to paint breeches on Michelangelo's Sistine nudes – for which he was ever afterwards known as *Daniele delle Braghe*, 'Daniel of the breeks'.

For most people, however, the picture which creates the strongest impression here is the *Deposition* by Rosso Fiorentino, painted in 1521. Rosso (1494–1541), thus nicknamed for his red beard, was a gloomy neurotic, whose manner continually alienated him from potential friends and patrons, both in Italy and France, where his work for King Francis I at Fontainebleau was abruptly ended by his suicide in remorse at his vindictive behaviour towards a rival. The turbulence here is compositional, in the restless pitching of long limbs and lurching ladders, the abjection of the red-gowned Magdalen slewed across the foot of the canvas, and the curved mourners on either side, one of them with a hint of incipient madness in her eyes.

From the gallery turn north to the city walls, where you gain an excellent view of the remains of a Roman theatre dating from the reign of Augustus, and third-century baths behind it. The area is still called Vallebuona, from a temple to the Bona Dea which once stood here. East of this, keeping within the walls, you may either go hunting more Roman and Etruscan traces in the archaeological museum in Via Marcoli, passing the church of Sant'Agostino, where the chapel of the Madonna delle Grazie was endowed by the Bolognese Count Felicini, one of the area's most notorious bandits, or inspect the huge *rocca* where he died in 1715 after 43 years' imprisonment, chained in a darkened cell. Built in two stages between the fourteenth and fifteenth centuries, the *rocca* is still a penitentiary, its western end known as 'La Femmina' (the woman) and the eastern tower called 'Il Maschio' (the man). It has played host to Tuscany's most distinguished prisoners, from contumacious renaissance noblemen to Risorgimento rebels and, in our own century, courageous anti-Fascists. Volterra itself, in the best sense, takes us prisoner: after a single visit it never lets us go.

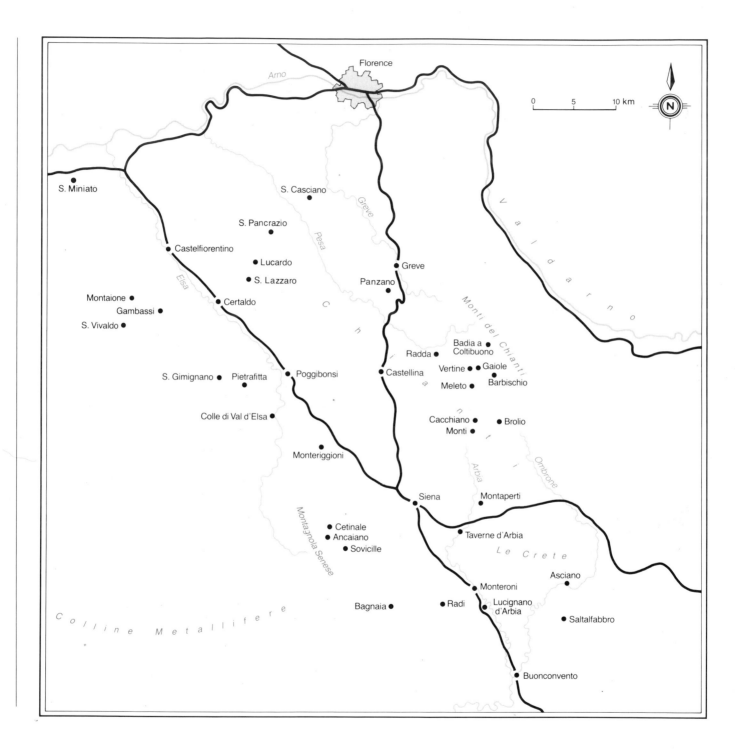

3
Siena and the Chianti

Siena – Asciano – Buonconvento –
Colle di Val d'Elsa – San Gimignano – San Vivaldo –
Certaldo – Castelfiorentino – San Miniato

For most people the typical Tuscan landscape is that of the undulating hill country between Florence and Siena known as the Chianti. Its particular clichés are almost too well known to need enumerating: the villa or the farmhouse on a hilltop, amid the grey clusters of olive trees and the dark files of cypresses (the classic Tuscan 'neighbour's landmark'), the serried vines streaking the slopes and the most intensely and continuously farmed fields in Europe.

For many, indeed, this is all the Tuscany they ever see or sometimes wish to see. Not for nothing is the country around Greve, Radda and Castellina known as 'Chiantishire', the territory of well-heeled English, whose expatriate rural seat is a converted *casa colonica*, the standard peasant house of the region, with swimming-pool attached. The only Italians they are likely to meet are the farmer's family at the bottom of the drive who do the cleaning and gardening: indeed, a member of this transplanted British gentry recently boasted to a magazine that he had no personal contact with the natives whatever and no desire to speak Italian.

Whether such a presence contributes much to the Chianti is doubtful, though you can understand why, once ensconced under the red pantiled loggia or draped around the poolside, the denizens of Chiantishire are unwilling to stir. This is a landscape of incomparably beautiful distances, enormous sweeps of gently folded hills framing horizons bounded by the ghostly cone of Monte Amiata to the south, the remote Apennines to the north and the shaven, scrubby uplands of the Maremma hinterland to the west. As the swallows cut the air in pursuit of the evening midges and the containing silence is so complete that you can hear the swish of their wings, it is scarcely any wonder that you should want to hold on to the moment rather than move away from it, except perhaps in search of food and drink.

The latter is the region's other enduring symbol – a pity, it always seems to me, since Chianti wine does not travel well, and whatever its merits, it is not the best in Italy. Attempts to impose an *appellation contrôlée* in the form of the DOC (*denominazione di origine controllata*) mean little in practice, but the Chianti has been more successful than some in maintaining standards. The area between Impruneta and Siena produces the *classico*, indicated by the black cock on the neck of the bottle. Elsewhere, in an area stretching almost to the gates of Florence, the *putto*, or little cherub, is the distinguishing mark, and the various vineyards,

Left **This urn stands in the garden of a villa near Castellina in Chianti.**

Above **The big granges of the *crete senesi*, the chalky uplands south of Siena.**

99

The elegant decorum of a war memorial at Castellina in Chianti.

several owned by the senior Florentine nobility, the Capponi, Frescobaldi, Antinori and others, arrest the traveller with their large roadside hoardings. The straw-covered bottles, which British newly-weds in the 1950s used to turn into lamps, are fast disappearing in favour of the standard claret shape, easier to pack and suggesting a wine to be taken seriously.

Such an innocent pursuit of happiness was not always the rule here. A territory constantly fought over by the rival powers of Florence and Siena, its people lived and died under the share-cropping system familiar throughout Italy until the present century and known as the *mezzadria*, a series of agreements between peasant and landowner which enabled the former to farm with materials the latter provided, the produce to be ultimately divided

between them. The various members of the farming family had their special names. At the head were the *capoccia*, who negotiated with the landowner, and his wife the *massaia*, who kept the house and supervised the feeding of the animals. The labourers were called *bifolchi*, and in some areas there was a peripatetic journeyman known as the *camporaiolo*. Everyone detested and feared the *fattore*, the bailiff who managed the estate.

The system worked better in theory than in practice. Successive changes in the law favoured the landlord, who had the right to break all agreements within a year. Since it was not in the farmer's interest to produce too much, most of the *poderi* (little holdings) afforded a basic subsistence. Fierce controversy among agronomists during the days of the Lorraine Grand Dukes produced no firm solution, and the *mezzadria* only started to run down in the decades after World War II, when most of the pretty farmhouse conversions now inhabited by British holidaymakers were abandoned by their original tenants in search of a better life in the towns.

The Chiantigiana, the road running down from Florence to Siena, is the region's only main highway, and it affords as good a glimpse as any of the immemorial patterns and colours of the landscape. The Chianti is not always attractive: its vineyards are now spiked with concrete stanchions looking, from a distance, like the graves in a military cemetery, and its treelessness often appears either boring or depressing. Yet there are always villages or little towns to turn aside into, like Greve, with its V-shaped arcaded Piazza del Mercatale, Panzano, stretched out along its hilltop, and Radda, still retaining traces of its role as headquarters of the Lega del Chianti, an autonomous group of Florentine frontier forts guarding the approaches from Siena. East of Radda you can drive to Badia a Coltibuono, with some of the most prized local vintages, and from here, turning south through Gaiole, you come upon several of the castles which pin down the folds of the landscape. Vertine, with its full girdle of ramparts, is perhaps the most beautiful, but Meleto, a medieval stronghold metamorphosed into a fortified farm, and Barbischio, a keep on top of a wooded hill, are just as eyecatchingly sited, while Brolio, even further south, is a memorial to the great Bettino Ricasoli (1809–80), one of the first prime ministers of united Italy, who turned a fort (in the family since 1141) into what looks rather like a Victorian country house.

This politician also lives on in a romantically sinister story – and it may only be a story – about him and his wife. Newly married, the dour young baron took his consort to her first Florentine ball and allowed her to be led to the dance-floor by a fellow nobleman, a distinctly eligible bachelor with several conquests to his credit. When the dance was over, Ricasoli announced to his wife that they were leaving, and ordered his coachman to drive at once to Brolio. It was a bitterly cold night and part of the journey took place under a driving blizzard, but the couple, freezing in their evening clothes, said nothing to one another. When they arrived, the baron treated his wife with every attention, while making it quite clear that she would never return to Florence. And she never did. And in their way they lived happily ever after.

From Brolio turn west, via Cacchiano and Monti, to rejoin the main road to Siena. The initial impact of the city, seen from a great distance in every direction, yet cunningly concealed within its cup of hills, never fails to grip those travelling towards it, and the promise made above the Porta Camollia, the gate on the Florence road, *Cor magis tibi Sena pandit* – 'Siena yet more readily spreads forth her heart to you' – is always in my experience stunningly fulfilled.

Perverse as such a partiality may seem, I find almost everything about Siena preferable to Florence. I respect and venerate Florence, but I love Siena. The

Religion and fantasy blend in this engaging detail from Via dei Pispini, Siena.

city's disposition, for a start, is infinitely sympathetic. Its dips, grooves and hollows are like those of a favourite old mattress into which it has rolled comfortably towards a dignified repose. The streets are all brick-paved, and brick, at its very warmest and most subtly-toned, is the dominant building material. Where stone does appear, it is seldom always of the same kind. When the German geologist Johann Joseph Ferber came here in 1776, the whole *sanese* region was a paradise to him. There were white, black, blue and green quartz, petrified shells, granite, travertine, green and black spotted serpentine, alabaster, malachite, agate, 'great white argillaceous and sulphureous bullets, some of the bigness of a man's head' and a beautiful yellow marble with black veins, known as *brocatello di Siena* – 'Siena brocade'.

101

The architecture, whether in the outer shell of the cathedral, so hated by Ruskin, or in the gothic palaces of nobles too proud to marry any but each other, so that by 1700 they needed papal dispensations to wed at all, has a fancy to it, a sense of narrative possibility, which is wholly Sienese in character. The city's very saints, Caterina Benincasa (1347–80) and Bernardino Albizzeschi (1380–1444) have this somewhat fanciful quality, not merely imagining another world but determined to bring it into being, yet never without a rough-hewn practicality, seldom reluctant to call a spade a spade.

Myth and legend imbued Siena from the outset. Nothing survives of the Roman Sena Julia, but the city's medieval inhabitants wanted to believe in its foundation by Senius and Ascius, sons of Remus, which is why the suckling she-wolf became the civic badge, seen wherever the republic held sway. Under the protection of the Holy Virgin, whose name was on all Sienese coins and traditionally invoked when any major crisis threatened the community, Siena profited from its position on two of the great thoroughfares of the Italian peninsula, the pilgrim route from France and the road which brought travellers from eastern Europe over the Apennines. Everyone fetched up sooner or later within its walls, emperors, popes, wandering saints, painters, sculptors and poets. Its super-efficient family banking firms were famous throughout Christendom, and a passionate loyalty to the city went hand in hand with a shrewd business sense.

'The Florentines and Senoys are by th'ears', says a Shakespearean lord, and Florence was the eternal rival. The Sienese believed that they alone were the guardians of liberty, and the word *libertas* was inscribed everywhere in their dominions. At the great battle of Montaperti, on 4 September 1260, Ghibelline Siena defeated Guelph Florence, the latter's rout owing something to the treachery of Bocca degli Abbati, who had cut off the hands of Jacopo della Narda, the Florentine standard-bearer. Though the Ghibelline triumph was short-lived, Siena herself consolidated her power and clung on to independence, until a ruinous series of early sixteenth-century wars, linked with the imperial ambitions of the Holy Roman Emperor Charles V, created desolation in her territories. The economic power-base of her ruling class was shattered, banditry was brought to the very gates and the city faced bankruptcy. Factionalism, looting and murder were rife by the time Charles and his vassal the Grand Duke Cosimo I of Tuscany blockaded the city, which held out for more than a year, from January 1554 to April 1555. Though the republican oligarchs retired, defiant, to Montalcino, it was a case of 'history to the defeated may say alas! but cannot help or pardon', and in 1559 Siena became part of the Grand Duchy, destined to live, like Venice, though without its melancholy introversion, on an illustrious past.

For most visitors the essence of this past is distilled by the elements of the Campo (the main square), one of the best known open spaces in Italy, perhaps because of its sheer exhilarating unorthodoxy. The shape itself, sloping and irregular, has never been successfully defined (an oyster, a fan, a spoon, a shoe?), but its surrounding palaces were deliberately intended to reflect an ideal social harmony, as laid down by the original order of the town's governors, the Nine, in 1297. And indeed they do, not so much by design as through colours and textures. For centuries the Campo has fulfilled the piazza's archetypal functions: fruit, fish and livestock were sold here, grain was handed out to the poor, San Bernardino preached his epic

---

The suckling she-wolf, symbol of Siena's legendary Roman foundation.

A touching detail from a sculpture in Palazzo Salimbeni, Siena.

sermons, felons were hanged, heretics were burnt and illustrious visitors were banqueted and entertained.

In this 'most beautiful square that can anywhere be found' the dominant building is the Palazzo Pubblico, from which medieval Siena was governed. Finished in 1310, it was further embellished with the chapel under Antonio Federighi's renaissance portico of 1468–70, built as a gesture of thanks for the passing of the Black Death in 1348. A more prominent addition was the dizzyingly slender tower 102 metres high known as the Torre del Mangia. The name derives from a spendthrift – *mangiaguadagni* – called Giovanni di Balduccio, whose job was to sound the great bell. The descendant of this instrument, cast in 1666, is known as Sunta from its dedication to Santa Maria Assunta.

The palace offers a good introduction to the idiosyncratic discourse of Sienese painting, a pleasing surprise to those arriving from Florence with heads full of Giotto and Fra Angelico. Sienese medieval art speaks to us in ways that Daddis and Gaddis cannot: the narrative romance, the decor, the sinuousness of line, the subtle tricks of colour, the affection intrinsic to the manner of masters such as Duccio (1255–1318), the Lorenzetti, Simone Martini (1284–1344) and others, are all irresistible. Look at Simone's *Maestà* (*Virgin in Majesty*) of 1315 in the Sala del Mappamondo, with the Virgin under her great canopy upheld by saints set against a deep blue ground, or at Vecchietta's *Saint Catherine* and Sano di Pietro's *San Bernardino* of about a century later in the same room, and you will find an extraordinary community of spirit among painters in a native tradition stretching right down to a splendid final flowering in Rutilio Manetti.

Designed to reflect such genius and the climate which fostered it, the frescoed walls of the Palazzo Pubblico concentrated as much on secular as on religious values. Nowadays visitors survey the painting of Guidoriccio da Fogliano (on the opposite wall of the Sala del Mappamondo to the *Maestà*) with a raised eyebrow. This equestrian portrait of the Sienese 'Captain of War' is attributed to Simone Martini and assigned to 1329, but there is now a gathering body of opinion which holds that the whole affair is an inspired fake intended to cover work by Sodoma lying underneath.

Most famous of all the palace frescoes are those in the Sala della Pace representing the allegorical figures of Good and Bad Government and their respective effects. These were carried out by Ambrogio Lorenzetti between 1337 and 1339 and include some of the most majestic and authoritative concepts of the Italian Middle Ages. Anybody writing about them is in danger of getting carried away (the best book on Siena, by Judith Hook, spends ten pages on them), so I reluctantly confine myself to a few general points. In our modern age of greedy, self-seeking individualism, it is a salutary shock to find Lorenzetti reflecting St Thomas Aquinas's philosophy of the common good, the basic bond of society, opposed to ruthlessness, treachery and discord, ruled by Fear, whose descriptive scroll bears the legend: 'Because he looks for his own good in the world, he places justice beneath tyranny. So nobody walks this road without Fear: robbery thrives inside and outside the city gates.'

Bad Government has, alas, deteriorated. Somehow it would, wouldn't it? But none of us can possibly forget Lorenzetti's pioneering treatment of landscape in *The Effects of Good Government*, in which the values of safety, prosperity and unity embodied by the walled city (clearly identified as Siena itself) are matched by the peace and order of the *contado*, where peasants till their fields and riders, huntsmen and merchants pass to and fro unmolested. That the Sienese took all this very seriously is proved by, among other things, the sermons San Bernardino preached on the frescoes, giving descriptions which have left us several valuable clues as to interpretation.

There is much more to see in the Palazzo Pubblico, including Taddeo di Bartolo's often neglected scenes from the life of the Virgin (1406–13) in the chapel, and some exceedingly colourful frescoes in the Sala del Risorgimento of famous moments in the nineteenth-century struggle for Italian unity. One of these ambitious works, all by local painters rising gamely to the challenge of their subject, shows the meeting between King Victor Emmanuel and Garibaldi on the road to Capua.

For proof that the Sienese are bound by a common sense of loyalty to their city greater than is shown anywhere else in Italy, you have only to be here on 2 July or 16 August to witness the *Palio*. This thrilling horse race around the sanded outer slope of the Campo constitutes the citizens' ultimate pledge of allegiance to the history and traditions which have nurtured them. More than Lorenzetti and Duccio and the floor of the *duomo*, more than the toothsome *panforte*, a cake of spice, nuts and candied peel topped with cinnamon, or the macaroons known as *ricciarelli*, it is the *Palio* that seduces the visitor, the intensity of the occasion transporting even the most high-minded and phlegmatic tourist.

The race to win the embroidered banner of the Holy Virgin is run between 10 of the city's 17 districts,

Sallustio Bandini, pioneer agronomist, carrying a message of hope to the Maremma, in the square named after him in Siena.

known as *contrade*, each of whose representative banners (the Tortoise, the Panther, the Owl etc.) is borne in procession around the course by costumed flag-wavers. In the early afternoon before the race, the horses of the competing *contrade* will have been blessed in their parish churches (a pile of droppings on the floor is viewed as a good omen) and the priest will pronounce the traditional words: 'Go, little horse, and return a winner!' When the race finally starts, it is amid an amazing atmosphere of violence, corruption and passion, as the jockeys shove, push and buffet one another, fights break out within the crowd, and there is pain, blood and even death – all for an event over in a few minutes. But the intense loyalties displayed are to the *contrada* itself, which every Sienese regards as a huge extended family. As a final paradox, I should point out that Siena has one of the lowest crime rates in Europe and that life on either side of the *Palio* is irreproachably sedate.

West out of the Campo, turn left and walk down Via di Città, past the fourteenth-century Palazzo Chigi Saracini on the left. It was from here that the victory of Montaperti was announced to the citizens by the drummer Ceccolini, who had watched the fight from the top of the tower. The palace now contains one of Italy's finest music academies and concerts are given here each summer. Nearly opposite stands Palazzo Piccolomini, begun in 1460 to designs by Bernardo Rossellino as a residence for Caterina Piccolomini. She was the sister of Pope Pius II, so her house is known as '*delle papesse*' – 'of the she-popes'.

Turning right up Via del Capitano, you come to the *duomo*, one of the most frequently painted of Italian buildings because it seemed to Sienese artists to

---

The *duomo* of Siena, with an arch of the unfinished fourteenth-century cathedral to its left.

express the ultimate significance of their city. The decorated gothic façade of 1376, by Giovanni di Cecco, is deceptive: if you look closely, you will see that the lower arches of the doorways and their pillars are in fact romanesque and very late at that, the work of Giovanni Pisano, completed in 1299. Between these two stages, the ruling Nine conceived a grandiose project for an entirely new cathedral, intended as the most magnificent in Italy, but work was broken off by rising costs and, more seriously, by the advent of the Black Death.

What we have today, an embellishment of Pisano's existing work, is by any standards one of the most immediately compelling of the world's religious buildings and its grip on generations of travellers has been irresistible. Wagner loved it, seeing it as a perfect setting for *Parsifal*. The Russian poet Aleksandr Blok, writing in 1909, saw it as an embodiment of our fears of the life to come, while Joseph Addison, two hundred years earlier, was moved, in an age not noted for its interest in medieval art, to exclaim 'There is nothing in this city so extraordinary as the cathedral, which a man may view with pleasure after he has seen St Peter's, though it is of quite another make, and can only be looked upon as one of the masterpieces of gothic architecture.'

When you have finished reeling in amazement at the stonework stripes stretching from floor to ceiling in the nave and aisles, which transform the cathedral into a giant mint humbug, and at the busts of popes and emperors above the arches, look down at the floor, whose marble intarsia paving, begun in 1376, was only finished in 1562. There is nothing to match it anywhere else. In the checkerwork of inlaid stone, its white marble designs picked out in black stucco, the labour of various hands, including those of Domenico Beccafumi (1486–1551), Giacomo Cozzarelli (1453–1515) and Matteo di Giovanni (1435–95), can be seen in a singular combination of biblical narrative, allegory

107

and holy wisdom, with depictions of anything from the symbols of Siena's subject towns to the four sybils who supposedly foretold Christ's coming.

The high altar itself is an ideal ensemble of renaissance craftsmanship, devised and positioned by Pandolfo Petrucci, virtual dictator of Siena in the early sixteenth century, using elements of an altar originally under the dome – a canopied shrine by Vecchietta, two angels by Francesco di Giorgio and eight others below by Beccafumi. On the walls of the apse behind are some remarkably appealing frescoes showing *Esther and Ahasuerus* and *The Israelites in the Wilderness*, by Ventura Salimbeni (1567–1613), a painter who deserves more than the tactful mention he usually gets. To the left of the altar, Nicola Pisano's pulpit, of 1265–8, provides a remarkably ornate counterpart to similar work in the Pisa baptistery, and some may feel that in concept and execution it is an altogether more sophisticated achievement. Beyond this, amid the frescoes by Pinturicchio (1454–1518) on the walls of the chapel of San Giovanni Battista in the north transept, you will find a superb statue of the lean, ascetic Baptist himself, a late work by Donatello, dated 1457. It is impertinent of me, after the great Florentine, to ask you to notice the monument further down the north aisle to the Sienese patrician Marcantonio Zondadari, but I love this periwigged portrait bust and always shall. It was executed in 1725 by Giuseppe and Bartolomeo Mazzuoli, and very handsomely they did it too.

You are now near the entrance to a unique feature of the cathedral and one of the loveliest things in all Siena, the library built by Cardinal Francesco Piccolomini (later Pope Pius III) in 1495 to house the books collected by his uncle Aeneas Sylvius

Part of the superb inlaid pavement of the *duomo* at Siena.

Piccolomini, Pope Pius II, who had died in 1464. Aeneas Sylvius was a renaissance man down to the very Latinizing of his name, and his dreams and ambitions fused all the strands of romantic idealism essential to the spirit of the age. Born in 1405, he led a merry youth, with much poetry and many women, before embarking upon a career as a diplomat which sent him on missions to England, Scotland and Germany. When he finally took holy orders, his talent and energy were irresistible – in a few years he was Bishop of Trieste, Cardinal of Siena and at last, as the Italians say, *papabile* – 'popable' – becoming Supreme Pontiff in 1456. Alas, his papacy was neither glorious nor especially happy, and when he finally succeeded in raising a Crusade to recapture Constantinople, it was rumoured that the Crusaders, ready to embark at Ancona where he had arrived to bless them, had arranged to poison him so as to sidestep their obligations.

The Piccolomini library is both a typical act of Sienese family piety and a celebration of a crowded life. Its walls are frescoed by Pinturicchio with a sequence of episodes evoked with an extraordinary brilliance, verve and lavishness of detail. Fashionable as it has been to do this Perugian painter down ever since Bernard Berenson pitched into him at the turn of the century, it is worth asking how the subject in question could possibly have been handled with a more perfect sense of its context and background. Aeneas Sylvius would have adored the sumptuous classical decor, the exuberance of Pinturicchio's palette and the theatrically posed scenes of homage and ceremony, including the embassy to King James III in a romantically wild Scotland. Three nude Greek Graces from the third century BC in the middle of the room suggest the flourish of a renaissance signature across the entire ensemble.

Turn left outside the *duomo* and walk along the south side of the building, from which you can see all

St Peter and St Paul, fifteenth-century statues by Vecchietta on Siena's Loggia della Mercanzia.

that remains of the immense but all too flimsy project for the new cathedral, a set of transept arches by Lando di Pietro and Domenico di Agostino, left eternally unfinished in 1355. These now shelter the Museo dell'Opera del Duomo, containing stonework and pictures formerly in the cathedral. Those interested in Italian sculpture will make for Giovanni Pisano's nobly conceived saints, or for Jacopo della Quercia's expressive relief showing St Jerome presenting Cardinal Casini to the Virgin and Child, in which the fervour of each countenance is matched by a delicacy in the modelling of hands and draperies. On the first floor is the great *Maestà*, painted by Duccio di Buoninsegna between 1308 and 1311 for the high altar, but shamefully dismembered during the eighteenth

century. The large central panel of the *Virgin in Majesty* that remains, however, with 26 scenes from Christ's Passion on its reverse, is enough to make this work a statement of infinite resonance in the art of the world.

Duccio, like all medieval Sienese painters, was intensively engaged in the communal life of the city (one of his jobs, for example, was looking for additional water supplies) and this sense of a shared tradition, consolidated by social and family relationships, imbues Sienese art across the centuries. For a superb demonstration of such unity of feeling, turn out of the cathedral square, down Via del Capitano and into Via San Pietro, where the crenellated gothic Palazzo Buonsignori holds my favourite Tuscan gallery. What is it about Sienese painting that endlessly excites our affection and indulgence, even towards somebody like Sano di Pietro (1406–81), of whom the panjandrums tell us we should not think too highly? Sano's work perhaps especially sums it all up, with his sense of humour, fallibility and coarse rustic charm. Notice the donkey's rump as it enters the city gate in his *Madonna appearing to Calixtus III*, or the wattle fencing and homely garb of the shepherds in the predella panel of one of his altarpieces. The same humanity surrounds the ploughmen and diggers in the background of Giovanni di Paolo's *Flight into Egypt*, the rich caparisons and neighing horses of Bartolo di Fredi's *Adoration of the Magi*, and the little panels which are all the city possesses by the sublime Sassetta, most admired Sienese painter of his period.

From Palazzo Buonsignori, return to Via di Città and follow it as far as the elegant Teatro dei Rozzi (1816, by Alessandro Doveri), turning left into Piazza dell' Indipendenza. A sharp left off Via delle Terme from

The early baroque church of Santa Maria di Provenzano, Siena.

A charming detail from a fountain in the courtyard of Palazzo Salimbeni, Siena.

the saint and some excellent canvases by Sienese baroque painters.

Leave the city by the road to Arezzo and turn off towards Taverne d'Arbia. You are now out in the Sienese *contado*, whose landscape in this area takes on a highly distinctive look recalled from the backgrounds of predella panels and other medieval paintings. These chalk outcrops, bony elbows and ankles sticking out of the flesh of the eroded soil, are known as the *Crete* (*creta* is the Italian for chalk) and they form a hauntingly barren prospect of rolling, treeless wolds, yellow for harvest in summer, grey ploughland in winter, with comparatively few villages and a sprinkling of large, squat farms like blockhouses looking warily across the ridges towards Monte Amiata.

In their midst is unassuming little Asciano, acquired by Siena in 1285. If you go all the way up the Corso Matteotti, the pleasant main street of the town, you will find steps at the end of it leading to the Collegiata, whose simple romanesque façade I far prefer to the liquorice allsort churches from the same period further north. Most of the best paintings from here and elsewhere in Asciano have been shifted to the oratory on the north side of the church, which is now the town museum. There are two fine early works by Matteo di Giovanni and a *Madonna and Child* by Ambrogio Lorenzetti, but the most memorable visual experience is surely *The Birth of the Virgin* by the unknown fifteenth-century genius referred to as the Master of the Osservanza. This picture, with its magical blend of the homely and the spiritual, reflects the essentially public nature of medieval childbirth. Angels may be hovering, since it is none other than St Anne who is in

here brings you to the house of St Catherine in Via del Tiratoio. In the course of her short life, Caterina Benincasa stamped her remarkable personality on the world of the late fourteenth century. Joining the order of widows known as the Mantellate in 1363, when she was 15, she ministered to the poor and sick, earning a reputation for exemplary acts of pious charity and self-denial. A year or so later she managed to prevent a war between the Tuscan cities and the Pope, and in 1376 she persuaded the Holy Father to return to Rome from Avignon, where Clement V, a Frenchman, had removed the Papacy in 1309. By the time of her death, aged only 33, she had achieved international fame as a peacemaker, and her letters to kings and prelates in this cause have a wondrously powerful simplicity. Her house, now an extensive sanctuary, contains relics of

Evening in the valley of the Ombrone, near Asciano.

labour, but there are plenty of sensible women with water and towels to see that all goes smoothly.

Turn south now, along the minor road via Santa Lucia and Saltalfabbro, to the Benedictine abbey of Monte Oliveto Maggiore, whose somewhat barrack-like appearance should not put you off. The place was deliberately chosen for its wild solitude by the learned Sienese nobleman Bernardo Tolomei, who was convinced, after an attack of blindness during a philosophy lecture in 1313, that he must found not only a monastery but an order besides. Both still exist, though the abbey no longer functions as a monastic institution. There is much to enjoy here, from the seventeenth-century chemists' jars of the pharmacy to the illuminated missals of the library and the wooden inlay of the choir-stalls (1503–05) by Giovanni da Verona in the late baroque church of 1772. Noblest survivors of all, however, are the frescoes adorning the great cloister, painted between 1497 and 1505 by Luca Signorelli and Giovanni Antonio Bazzi, known as Il Sodoma (1477–1549).

Their commissioned theme was the life of St Benedict, from his schooldays in Rome to his miracles as the founder of monasticism. Signorelli, whom you will meet at Cortona, painted nine of the central episodes with his exalted, visionary buoyancy of touch, and it was Sodoma's job to complete the sequence on either side. He was a genuine eccentric, whose oddities fascinated everyone even as they lifted pious hands in horror at the unconventional life which earned him his nickname. Vasari's biography makes him appear quite irresistible, with his menagerie of pets (including a tame raven he had taught to imitate him) 'insomuch that the dwelling of this man seemed like Noah's Ark', and his eternal readiness to enjoy jokes against himself. He was born at Vercelli in Lombardy, but the Sienese took him to their hearts and made much of him, and we too are beginning to appreciate his genius as a joyous, sensual colourist,

reflected in these frescoes which it would be a sin to dismiss, as one philistine Edwardian wrote them off in 1906, as 'drab-coloured, flabby inanity . . . boys, baggages and spiritual erotics'. Sodoma had a sense of humour, that was all, and the monks, who called him *Il Mattaccio* – 'the big madman' – learned to love the young sinner with his raffish entourage of 'colour-grinders'.

From Monte Oliveto go straight on down to Buonconvento, within its low, machicolated town walls. It was here that the Ghibelline champion Henry VII, Holy Roman Emperor, met his death on 24 August 1312, either from sheer exhaustion having spent the previous week energetically wrecking villages, or from a poisoned wafer at the mass. The jubilant Guelphs rang the bells, but Dante, who had hoped he would fall on Florence, was made yet more wretched by the death of the man who, his poetry had prophesied, would come 'to straighten out Italy before she was prepared for it'.

You enter the town by a sturdy medieval gate, with a little nineteenth-century theatre next to it and the church of San Pietro e Paolo beyond. The palace immediately opposite holds, as at Asciano, a collection of paintings gathered from various churches, none of them especially distinguished, but an absorbing witness to the diffusion of Sienese art through the city's own territory.

Buonconvento was a staging-post for travellers to Rome before the arrival of the railway. Lady Morgan spent a miserable night here in 1817, with smelly bedclothes, fleas and 'the blasts that whistled through the manifold chinks of the room', while Tobias Smollett, in 1761, was plagued by a rascally innkeeper to whom he had refused a tip and who, in revenge,

Storm clouds gather over a farmhouse in the Sienese countryside.

harnessed two unbroken stallions to his carriage. This is the classic old road to the south, its stones steeped in the thrills and vexations of a thousand years of journeying foreigners, and I can never pass along it without a lifting of the spirits, almost hearing the crack of the coachman's whip as he drives Dickens, Mendelssohn, Berlioz or Horace Walpole down the dusty highway. The low hills on either side are crowned with some of the most beautiful of all Italian farmhouses, big brown granges looking as though they had been placed there as eyecatchers by a passing landscape architect, and the little fortified village of Lucignano d'Arbia, to be taken in as you go north towards Siena, has an overwhelmingly painterly quality about its walls and windows.

Just before you reach Monteroni, turn left via Radi and Bagnaia and then go up towards Sovicille. North of here – you are now in the zone known as the Montagnola Senese – is the beautifully dignified parish church of Ancaiano, sixteenth-century work of considerable stylishness, with a dome and cupola. I wish I knew who the architect was. Still keeping north, you come to Cetinale, where the villa designed by Carlo Fontana in 1680 for Cardinal Fabio Chigi, surrounded by its ornamental garden jocularly called 'La Tebaide' after the early Christians' famous Egyptian hermitage, gives an excellent notion of the *villeggiatura* of a Sienese noble family. A little to the north you catch sight of many-towered Monteriggioni, which looks more impressive from a distance than it seems at close quarters. Fortified in 1219, it guarded the northern approaches to Sienese territory and fended off a Florentine attack in 1254. Dante made it the subject of a famous simile, when he compared an abyss full of giants in the *Inferno* to the castle of Monteriggioni. After its capture by the Grand Duke's forces in 1554 it was allowed to decline and is now merely a charming fortified village – a fangless lion if ever there was. With distant eastward glimpses a few

kilometres to the north of the castle of Staggia, you finally reach Colle di Val d'Elsa, which, like Massa Marittima further south, is divided into an upper and lower town.

Colle was the scene, in 1269, of the battle in which the Florentines gained their long-awaited revenge for Montaperti. With an almost lunatic courage, they hurled themselves into the midst of a vastly superior Sienese force, routing both horse and foot. Its commander, Provenzano Salvani, was taken prisoner, but his personal enemy Cavolino Tolomei stole into the camp, cut off his head and placed it on his lance. Another with a private grudge was the Sienese woman Sapia, whom Dante placed in Purgatory for exulting over her city's defeat as she watched the rout from a nearby tower.

There is still much from the period of the battle here, spread out across the ridges and valleys which orchestrate thoroughfares and buildings. In the lower town is the perpetually unfinished church of Sant'Agostino, with an interior redesigned two hundred years later by Antonio da Sangallo, but it is in Colle Alta that the Dantesque savour rises to meet you from medieval walls and gates, the mishmash of fresco in the style of the Lorenzetti in the Bishop's Palace and the tower which belonged to the great architect Arnolfo di Cambio, born here around 1250.

This is an ideal place in which to prepare yourself for the great object of this part of the journey, seen in a breathtaking first glimpse by taking the Volterra road as far as Le Grazie. What is it, perched with such obviously dramatic effect on the far hilltop? A beached ship stripped of spars and sails, or, as one writer aptly calls it, 'a tipsy miniature New York'?

Colle Alta is the oldest part of the town of Colle di Val d'Elsa, north-west of Siena.

San Gimignano has somehow endured as the perfect Tuscan medieval town, and though doubtless more appealing in the days of E. M. Forster, who made it the setting, as Monteriano, for his *Where Angels Fear to Tread*, it has successfully overcome the potential shocks of mass tourism and retained its character against all odds. Henry James described it as 'presenting itself more or less in the guise of some rare silver shell, washed up by the sea of time, cracked and battered and dishonoured, with its mutilated marks of adjustment to the extinct type of creature it once harboured figuring against the sky as maimed gesticulating arms flourished in protest against fate'. He means, of course, the famous towers, the '*Belle Torri*', of which there used to be nearly eighty: now only 13 remain. There are other tall towers in Italy, but these are the ones everybody remembers. Built as fortresses, they were places of refuge for the adherents of two warring families, the Guelph Ardinghelli and the Ghibelline Salvucci, whose civil strife played right into the hands of Florence, which assumed control in 1354.

The city took its name from the Modenese bishop Geminianus, whose aid was happily invoked when Attila's Huns threatened attack in AD 450, and its subsequent prosperity owed a good deal to the wool trade and a spice market which sent saffron, cloves and pepper to Genoa and Naples. Dante came here on a Florentine embassy in 1300, Savonarola spent some time as a monk in the Dominican convent, and Machiavelli established a local militia. The industrious local historian Canon Pecori, writing in 1850, notes that the city fathers, with solicitous prudence, 'to avoid greater evils', established a municipal brothel in 1328, an institution maintained, it seems, until the close of the eighteenth century. Was this common practice in Tuscany or unique to San Gimignano?

Entering from the south, go up Via San Giovanni until you reach Piazza della Cisterna, named from the central thirteenth-century well. The whole *mise-en-scène* is medieval, with two splendid Ardinghelli towers on the north side. From here you enter the cathedral square, which has no less than seven towers, and you can choose whether to climb that of the Palazzo del Podestà, of 1337, or the even larger one attached to the Palazzo del Popolo. From either there are stupendous prospects across the hill country of western Tuscany, but even more impressive views into the town itself, with little terrace gardens here and

San Gimignano watches over the town he saved from the Huns, which bears his name.

Left **San Gimignano's memorable skyline of medieval towers can be seen from far away across the Tuscan hills.**

Above **Under an archway in San Gimignano.**

Opposite page **The medieval Collegiata is the cathedral church of San Gimignano.**

there, and outcrops of wallflower and houseleek chequering the old stones.

The cathedral itself, the Collegiata, was rebuilt by the Florentine architect Giuliano da Maiano (1432–90) and is one of the most richly frescoed churches in Italy. Barna da Siena did the New Testament scenes in the south aisle, but died while finishing them in 1351 when he fell from the scaffolding. His fellow citizen Bartolo di Fredi complemented these with an Old Testament sequence on the opposite side, begun ten

years later. Most attractive of all the cycles, however, is that decorating the chapel of Santa Fina, designed in 1468 by Giuliano da Maiano and his brother Benedetto as an eloquently graceful shrine to a local saint. Fina de Ciardi was a poor nobleman's daughter whose belief that her mysterious illness was a divine judgment caused her to spend five years lying on her back in expiation of her sins, at the close of which she died. Since she refused to move even for the purposes of nature, the circumstances of her decline may be imagined. Worms and mice feasted on her while still alive, but at her death (she was 15) a miraculous fragrance perfumed the house and the bells of the city rang of themselves. Her story is told on the chapel walls by Domenico Ghirlandaio with all the charm and sentiment at his command. Notice, for example, the beatific innocence transfiguring the scene at Fina's funeral, where her old nurse Beldia's maimed hand is healed and a monk, touching the saint's feet, regains his sight.

One of the joys of San Gimignano is the wealth of fine painting crammed within its walls. In the Palazzo del Popolo, where Dante addressed the chief citizens on his embassy, there is a grandiose frescoed *Maestà* by the Sienese artist Lippo Memmi, signed and dated 1317, and on the floor above is the municipal gallery, the best of whose collection, for me at least, is the wonderfully gawky, anguished *Crucified Christ*, with scenes from the Passion in small panels, by Coppo di Marcovaldo, who worked in Florence during the thirteenth century. There are several examples here by the hand of Benozzo Gozzoli (1420–97), one of whose most ambitious achievements can be seen north along Via San Matteo.

Gozzoli is one of those second division renaissance masters, like Filippino Lippi, Sodoma and Fra Bartolomeo, about whom the world chooses to be snooty. I have never been able to understand why, since the man could paint, and his lively handling of colour and decorative elements of costume and landscape was second to none. He worked extensively at San Gimignano and must often have walked along Via San Matteo, so 'suggestive', so 'characteristic' as Italian guidebooks say, in its unbroken ensemble of medieval palaces, towers and courtyards. The choir in the gothic church off to the right of Via San Matteo in Piazza Sant'Agostino is entirely covered with a treatment of the story of St Augustine.

We know from an inscription on the seventh fresco from the left, on the lowest band, that these seventeen opulent, vividly evoked scenes were commissioned by Fra Domenico Strambi, 'a famous doctor of the University of Paris', in 1464. The human touches here, as in Ghirlandaio's depiction of Santa Fina, are what captivate the spectator – St Augustine's mother praying for him, his vision of a child trying to empty the sea with a cup (a symbol of the vanity of trying to fathom the mysteries of the Trinity) and the boy saint being given a beating at school.

There is something in all this which strikes an echo from one of the town's earlier geniuses, the poet Folgore di San Gimignano, who died around 1316. He spent much of his life in Siena, where he was part of a fashionable clique of young men whom Dante was later to refer to as 'the spendthrift brigade', frittering their money away on fine clothes, hunting dogs and horse harness. Here he wrote a sequence of beautiful sonnets on the months of the year which are like little windows into the daily life of medieval Tuscany. They drank deeply, this '*brigata spendereccia*', and some of their cups would surely be of the golden-hued Vernaccia, best of Tuscany's white wines, produced around the village of Pietrafitta to the east of San Gimignano.

You now have a choice between the hermitage of San Vivaldo and Boccaccio's home town of Certaldo. Whatever you decide, the country between San Gimignano and the Arno valley is among the loveliest of the entire region, empty of large towns and major roads, gently hilly, softened with olives and stretches of broom and bracken, and without that laundered, hairbrushed look that so spoils the Chianti. There are marvellous romanesque churches too, at Pieve a Chianni near Montaione, San Pancrazio and San Lazzaro a Lucardo along the road to San Casciano, which is part of a remote farm with hens and geese running about the courtyard (the door was unlocked for me on my last visit by a withered crone with an orange beard).

San Vivaldo, which you reach by the western fork of the road north, is always worth the journey. Tucked deep into the forest of Boscolazzeroni, it was founded in 1300 as a retreat by Vivaldo Stricchi, a Franciscan friar who died in great holiness in the hollow of a chestnut tree, although the present convent dates from

---

A harmony of brick and stone in Piazza Pecori, San Gimignano.

the beginning of the sixteenth century. It was here that three friars, Cherubino, Tommaso and Mariano, instituted the sequence of 34 pilgrim chapels (there are now only 17) designed to reproduce the Christian sanctuaries of the Via Dolorosa in Jerusalem. Travellers in the far north of Italy will know of the Sacri Monti of Varallo and Oropa laid out in this fashion, with each little chapel featuring a scene from the Passion story in painted terracotta, but the San Vivaldo series is unique in Tuscany. Works of exceptional eloquence and dramatic simplicity, the best of them is the *Madonna dello Spasimo*, capturing that terrible moment when the Virgin, seeing her son staggering under the weight of his cross, sank into the arms of her companions.

Turning east, via Montaione and Gambassi, you reach Certaldo, where the old town lies along a gently sloping hilltop. Giovanni Boccaccio, whose statue stands in the main square of the lower town, and whose house, much restored and mournfully empty, is on the south side of the street named after him within the medieval walls, was not actually born here, but in Paris in 1313. It was his father's family who came from Certaldo, and though Boccaccio spent much of his youth enjoying the good life of Naples – a city whose inhabitants know all about the good life – he returned to Tuscany in middle age to produce that masterly series of literary works which fired the imagination of Chaucer and Shakespeare, culminating in the great collection of tales entitled *Il Decamerone*. In 1363, he settled permanently at Certaldo and is buried in the church of SS Michele e Iacopo at the end of the street. And a very pretty street this is, paved with diamonds of brick and sweeping you up to the medieval Palazzo Pretorio, encrusted with coats of arms and enclosing a most engaging little arcaded courtyard.

Go north along the main Empoli road now, to Castelfiorentino, by no means an especially attractive place but blessed with one gem in the shape of the church of Santa Verdiana, standing in a lopsided square in front of a large primary school. Late baroque is so unexpected in Tuscany that this majestic affair, with volutes on the central pediment and a handsome portico, is to be treasured. The architect was Bernardo Fallani, whose work here in 1771 carried on the tradition begun inside by Alessandro Gherardini and Lorenzo del Moro, responsible for the early eighteenth-century frescoes and stucco work, which have recently been given a magnificent restoration.

Santa Verdiana (1178–1242) was a poor girl of the town, whose early reputation for piety was increased when she entered the little cell you can see right under the church, where she dwelt for 34 years, taking as her companions two serpents, whom she fed daily until the foolish citizens killed them. She was visited by no

The coat of arms of a sixteenth-century governor of Certaldo.

The grand fountain of the Naiads in Empoli's
Piazza Farinata is by Lorenzo Pampaloni (1827).

SIENA AND THE CHIANTI

Left **The varied greens and sentinel cypresses of the Tuscan landscape, as in this view near San Miniato, have inspired painters for centuries.**

Above **A screen of poplars in the countryside near San Miniato.**

less a man than St Francis, who made her a member of his order. The presence of the snakes may indicate a folk memory of some ancient pre-Etruscan cult, but, goddess or saint, Verdiana lies in a silver shrine in the north aisle of this most delightful ecclesiastical surprise.

North through the slightly dismal Elsa valley, the road takes you almost to Empoli, but you should now turn left and then left again up to San Miniato. Nobody has really 'cracked' this town in the way that towns like Montepulciano or San Gimignano have been opened up by travellers, and the result is a place of singular fascination, not least because of its odd layout. High up on a triangular hill falling steeply away into the valley of the lower Arno, San Miniato basically consists of three open spaces, each with an entirely distinctive character, reflecting its long-diminished grandeur and importance. For this was the metropolis of the imperial vicars, deputies of Holy Roman Emperors, several of whom visited the town in person. Countess Matilda of Tuscany herself was born here in 1046, and Frederick II built the citadel, of which only a single much-restored tower survives, in 1218. And another emperor, Napoleon, came here to visit an elderly priest by the name of Bonaparte whom he believed was the last of the original stock from which his Corsican family sprang.

The lopsided Piazza del Popolo is dominated by the unfinished façade of San Domenico, rebuilt in 1330 and crammed with decently unremarkable Tuscan art from the past five centuries. The exception is the admirably modelled tomb of the Florentine doctor Giovanni Chellini, not by Donatello, as often supposed, but by Pagno di Lapo Portigiani, using the more famous master's model. If you turn up Via Ser Ridolfo you will find some fine renaissance palaces, but still more rewarding is to go from the other end of the square along Via Augusto Conti and under an arch, which leads into Piazza della Repubblica. Like Palazzo dei Cavalieri in Pisa, the long façade of the seminary on the right-hand side is decorated with *sgraffito* patterns, the work of Lodovico Cardi, better known by the name of Cigoli, the village just to the west where he was born in 1559. The lower part of this building is a series of medieval shops, perhaps the only ones now surviving in Tuscany.

A flight of steps leads up to the Prato del Duomo, a tree-shaded garden with splendid views up the distant river towards the mountains. The *duomo* itself is dedicated to Saint Genesius, the patron saint of actors (he had started out in the profession) and is much restored and altered romanesque work, with a floridly gilt baroque ceiling. Next door is the diocesan museum, with a *Crucifixion* by Filippo Lippi and a terracotta Christ by Verrocchio (1435–88) among its treasures. Beyond this you can climb Frederick's tower, where jealous courtiers contrived to have poor Pier della Vigna, the Emperor's treasurer, imprisoned and blinded. He took his own life in despair and Dante placed him in his infernal suicides' wood, turning his hair into a tree where the harpies nested. Below the tower stands the imposing bulk of the early eighteenth-century Santuario del Crocifisso – hardly ever open, alas.

Elegant sixteenth-century mural decoration above medieval shopfronts in Piazza della Repubblica, San Miniato.

4
The Maremma and Southern Tuscany

Grosseto – Parco Naturale della Maremma –
Orbetello – Isola del Giglio – Isola di Giannutri –
Manciano – Pitigliano – Abbadia San Salvatore –
Arcidosso – Paganico – Montalcino – Castiglione
d'Orcia – San Quirico d'Orcia

The seventeenth-century Florentine poet Vincenzo da Filicaia wrote a famous sonnet in which he lamented Italy's 'fatal gift of beauty', which drew down upon her the tyranny and greed of other nations. Anyone journeying across Tuscany will understand exactly what he meant, but at least one region of the province seems designed to offset the notion that the whole area is a bland paradise crammed with Pieros and Botticellis, full of minor fifteenth-century altarpieces, romanesque cathedrals and rustic restaurants serving *pappardelle alla lepre* – pasta with hare sauce – to tourists with their heads full of Berenson and Vasari.

Italians often talk of 'correcting' their coffee with a dash of grappa or some other liqueur. The Maremma exists to correct Tuscany. It is not especially beautiful; large expanses of it are treeless, flat and boring, there are very few towns of any compelling interest and their appearance is sometimes ugly, dismal, even a trifle hostile. Yet Tuscany needs the Maremma so as to achieve completeness. We cannot know what it all means until we have heard the sea breezes rasping across those bald hillsides, through those interminable pine woods and over the staring green and yellow of the plains.

The Maremma's quintessential melancholy derives from the fact that it was once so very different. In Roman times this was the burgeoning, fat farmland of the *latifundia*, where a slave economy underpinned the huge estates of wealthy proprietors. With the fall of the empire the region gradually became a deserted swamp, as the coastline silted up, agriculture and most kinds of settled habitation were abandoned, pirate raids chased the remaining inhabitants towards the hilly hinterland and finally, around 1500, malaria arrived to scourge the whole area for nearly four centuries.

Gradually two distinct worlds began to take shape. During the summer months the herdsmen of great flocks of sheep and cattle took their beasts to the mountain pastures, followed by the inhabitants of towns and villages in the plain, who found work in the harvest fields around the fortified *borghi* of Monte Amiata. In the winter everyone returned, followed by a mass of pathetically poor miners and woodcutters from the zone known as the Colline Metallifere, with its mercury and borax deposits, who could eke out their incomes as day-labourers on the scattered ranches of the littoral. Even the public institutions of Grosseto followed this pattern, and every summer until 1897 the seat of regional administration shifted, for the malarial season, to the healthier air of Scansano, in the hills to the south-east.

Little of the more grinding poverty has endured. The *bonifica* begun on the admirable initiative of Grand Duke Leopold II during the early nineteenth century (he even instituted a rudimentary form of health service, with free quinine for malaria sufferers) was completed after World War II, when sweeping agrarian reforms destroyed the basis of the bad old system which had prevailed since the Middle Ages. The *casali*, big farmhouses containing a number of peasant families, have been knocked into smart new flats, though innovation of this sort inevitably has its critics.

There are still ranches and cowboys in the Maremma, however, though not all of them are dedicated to cattle-herding. The flat open country is excellent for riding, and much of it, especially on the high inland plateaux around Pitigliano, has been given over to what is known as *agriturismo*, in which city-dwellers, dressed, of course, in the smartest and most expensive hacking gear, can try out their horsemanship as part of an initial, long-delayed peacemaking between Italy and her countryside.

Many equestrians converge annually for the trotting races on Grosseto, capital of the Maremma. Heavily bombed during 1943–4, it is not the most attractive of Italian cities, but its ancient nucleus, within a complete girdle of ramparts begun in 1564 by Baldassare Lanci, compensates for the dreariness of industrial plant and high-rise apartments beyond.

Do not be misled, however, by the façade of the *duomo* in Piazza Dante, almost totally reconstructed in the 1840s with the utmost taste and skill: the campanile is an early twentieth-century attempt to make the best of a bad job, brought about by the tampering of former ages. Within is one of those dismally voluminous church interiors found all too easily up and down Italy. Poking about in the gloom

you can find the chapel of the Madonna delle Grazie, to the left of the high altar, with a late fifteenth-century reredos by Antonio di Ghino and an *Assumption* of the same period by Matteo di Giovanni.

The diocesan museum, which used to be above the cathedral sacristy, has now been incorporated with the archaeological museum in the Palazzo del Liceo in Via Mazzini. The former, on the second floor of the sixteenth-century palace, holds some good Sienese paintings, including the much-loved *Madonna of the Cherries* by Sassetta, in fact a drastically cut-down version of a larger work but none the less memorable for its tender portrayal of the infant Jesus clutching at the Virgin's mantle as he bobs at a cherry. The archaeological section is given over to finds from Etruscan cities of the Maremma, such as Roselle, Populonia and Vulci.

North of the museum, in Piazza dell' Indipendenza, is the church of San Francesco, originally a Benedictine foundation which passed to the friars in the early fourteenth century. Around this time, or maybe a little earlier, Duccio, or somebody very like him, painted the sinewy crucified Christ hanging above the west door. Do not miss the cloister to the left of the church, with its stately well-head given by Duke Ferdinand in 1590 and known as the *pozzo della bufala* (well of the buffalo cow).

The rest of Grosseto can be pleasantly comprehended in a walk round the ramparts, preferably in that blessed Italian time which is the cool of the evening. The tree-shaded walks and gardens here were laid out by Leopold II, whose statue, showing him protecting prosperous Mother Maremma while crushing the serpent malaria beneath his heel, stands in the

---

The figures above the cathedral porch at Grosseto are nineteenth-century copies of Sienese originals.

Left **The red earth of the Maremma and young olive trees near Grosseto.**

Above **At Grosseto Grand Duke Leopold II gazes benignly at the Maremma, whom he has saved from malaria.**

square next to the cathedral. Poor '*Babbo Leopoldo*'! If ever a sovereign had good intentions towards his people he did, but old-fashioned benevolence could not save him from the march of history, and he went miserably into exile in 1860. As the ducal family left Florence never to return, the Florentines, with barely a hint of irony, wished them a pleasant journey, but when they halted at Fiesole for a last look and burst into tears, they found they had forgotten to bring any handkerchiefs to cry into. Leopold, born a Hapsburg, became a perpetual guest of Franz Josef, the Austrian Emperor, but remained Tuscan to the bone and wrote some moving Italian memoirs to prove it.

The sea is so close that it is worth going there at once. This is a very different coast from the more northerly stretch between Livorno and Piombino, wilder, more barren, less obviously tamed with resorts, and hence far more exciting. The *macchia*, that landscape of umbrella pines, broom, cystus and marram grass which typifies the coastal Maremma, stretches right down to the shore, and the scents of ozone and resin and the cicadas' metallic grating offer the requisite Mediterranean texture.

You would do well to avoid the Via Aurelia, however, the most dangerous thoroughfare in Italy, especially at the height of the holiday season during July and August. Keep to the minor roads via Montiano and Impostino until you reach Fonteblanda. Then follow the road around the little bay towards Talamone. This is still just about as unspoilt as any small medieval fishing village can possibly be in the days of mass tourism in a country where a month at the sea is a yearly ritual, but the smart yachtsmen have already got here, and sooner or later the luxury apartment buildings will arrive. The charm is nevertheless enhanced by a medieval fortress as grimly windowless as a cardboard box, and a scatter of decent fish restaurants, of which the best is probably La Buca di Nonno Ghigo in Piazza Garibaldi.

Garibaldi himself was here for three days in May 1860, when the secret expedition of a thousand men, *I Mille*, to conquer Bourbon Sicily involved bamboozling the Neapolitans into thinking that he was preparing an invasion of the Papal States. The port's land approaches are sheltered by the long, green ridge of the Monti dell' Uccellina, now a national park. Covered in dense pine forest, the hills, with their outcrops of grey rock, slope down to a shoreline of unravaged beauty, the authentic Mediterranean of a kind almost gone from these over-peopled coasts. Deer, wild boar, badgers, porcupines, goats and wild cats browse, prowl and burrow in the woods, and the *maremmano* cowboys round up the herds of cream-coloured cattle with the help of great white dogs. Closed at dusk, the park is traversible only on foot, no bad thing in car-obsessed Italy and a deterrent to the ring-top-can and plastic-bottle brigade.

A perilously straight stretch of the Via Aurelia carries you down to the three parallel spits of land, known as *tomboli*, leading on to the Argentario peninsula, once an island. The property in Roman times of the family of Enobarbus, known to Shakespeareans as the character with the most beautiful lines in *Antony and Cleopatra*, it took its name from their banking activities (*argentarii*). It now plays host to the super-rich of modern Rome, Milan and Turin, presided over by Italy's premier industrial dynasty, the Agnelli of Fiat fame.

Travellers should therefore be prepared for a good deal of 'keep out' and 'trespassers will', though, in compensation for all the *gross luxus*, unusual attention has been paid to the environment, violated only by a recent wave of forest fires, apparently deliberate arson designed to clear the way for buccaneer developers. Argentario is still overwhelmingly attractive, with beetling cliffs on its southern side, deciduous woods with stands of hornbeam, elm and maple on the central *massif*, and marvellous bathing almost everywhere.

Only one major road does the entire tour of the peninsula, and this is best reached via Orbetello, which occupies a little bulge on the central spit, with lagoons on either side. Anyone interested in the fortifications of different periods littering the Tuscan landscape need only come to Monte Argentario to find what is in effect an open-air museum of warlike architecture. Orbetello was, after all, capital of the Spanish *presidi*, a series of strongholds along the nearby coast controlled by Spain in compensation for having ceded Siena to the Grand Duke in 1555. This arrangement, whose political significance diminished as Spanish power grew weaker during subsequent centuries, lasted until 1815, but the inhabitants of Argentario seldom complained, as taxes were light and government generally mild.

Orbetello's grandiose triple-arched Porta del Soccorso has an undoubtedly Hispanic flavour and might do just as well in Madrid or Mexico City. The Spaniards rebuilt the cathedral during the mid seventeenth century, leaving the graceful travertine gothic west front of 1376. In the Corso Italia, south of here, try the excellent local eels served in the restaurants.

Those in search of scenic gastronomy had better strike westwards, off the causeway and on to Argentario itself, where the road most enjoyably hugs the coast, to reach Porto Santo Stefano, a place whose attractions neither wartime bombardment nor tourist assault have been wholly able to crush. Under the bastions of the fort, built by the enterprising governor Nuno Orejon, half the pleasure craft of Italy cram the harbour, and there is a wealth of good small *trattorie* in either direction. This is as suitable a base as any for exploring the peninsula's western fringes, eloquently rocky and deserted after the road gives up and turns inland at Cala Piccola to veer south again towards Port'Ercole. The latter is probably the most popular resort among the yachting glitterati, some of whom spend more time being photographed on their boats than actually sailing them.

There are no less than three Spanish forts here, all in splendid shape, two of them, the Forte Filippo and the Forte Stella, built to fend off possible repetitions of the attack by the Turks in 1543 under the dreaded admiral Kair-ed-Din Barbarossa. Not content with this, the Spaniards shored up the original Sienese *rocca* which essentially contains the ancient town, dedicated to Hercules by the Etruscans. To the north, along the strand of Tombolo di Feniglia, the painter Caravaggio died in 1610. Half distracted at the loss of his possessions during his flight from Papal justice after killing his opponent in a tennis match which became a brawl, he wandered by the shore in the blazing afternoon, to fall a victim to sunstroke and mortal fever.

Monte Argentario, as we have seen, was once part of the Tuscan archipelago, and it is by ferry from Porto Santo Stefano that you can reach two real islands, both with those genuine tinges of romantic possibility all islands ought to possess. The larger, Giglio, is still, by the skin of its teeth, free from what Italian guidebooks refer to with sinister vagueness as 'tourist equipment', though the bay of Campese on the west coast is starting to achieve the all-too-familiar *bijou* resort look. Nevertheless the sea is still clean, the myrtle, lentisk and cistus come down to the edge of the granite cliffs, and the cross-country walks (there is only one road) are of a beauty which makes you constantly wonder whether Ariel, Miranda or Caliban might deign to put in an appearance.

Giglio's story was not always an affair of 'sounds and sweet airs that give delight and hurt not'. The last poet of Roman antiquity, Rutilius Namatianus, describes the arrival here of refugees from the onslaught of the Goths in the fifth century, and the island was a continual prey for Moorish pirates: Barbarossa sent 700 inhabitants into slavery in 1544

and the navy of the Bey of Tunis was narrowly beaten off in a heroic resistance by the islanders in 1799. Perhaps the most fascinating of Giglio's owners was Countess Margherita Aldobrandeschi, originally married to Count Guy de Montfort, son of the famous Simon, champion of the English barons against Henry III. In revenge for his father's death Guy murdered Henry's son at mass in Viterbo cathedral north of Rome and inevitably found a place in Dante's *Inferno*.

Margherita herself began an affair with Nello de' Pannochieschi, the murderer of Pia di Tolomei, famously commemorated in that laconic epitaph in the *Purgatorio* '*Siena mi fe, disfecemi Maremma*' (Siena made me, Maremma unmade me). Not content with him, the insatiable countess went on to marry Orso Orsini and then, when he died, she gladly accepted Pope Boniface's suggestion of his nephew Lorenzo as a husband. Changing his mind, Boniface annulled the marriage, so Margherita turned for solace to her cousin Guido da Santafiora, but the Holy Father, accusing her of *fellonias et excessus enormes*, finally compelled her to do the decent thing and marry Nello. The wretched Guy de Montfort had died years earlier in an Aragonese gaol.

Now the island is a haven for wildlife outside the annual period of grotesque carnage which passes in Italy for 'hunting'. An exceptionally rich fauna includes buzzards, kestrels and peregrine falcons, the rare Sardinian toad and a carefully guarded colony of moufflon, the mountain sheep which have probably disappeared elsewhere in the Mediterranean. The field terraces are bright with scabius, coltsfoot and yarrow, and Giglio is in any case a botanist's delight, the only spot outside North Africa where you can find the wild mustard *sinapis procumbens* and the sole place in Tuscany to bloom with the pendent yellow flowers of artemisia.

By a happy coincidence, Artemisia was the ancient name of the tiny, cutlet-shaped island of Giannutri, reached by boat from Giglio. The Enobarbi had a villa here as well, on the northern coast (the remains can be visited), but cultivation only returned to Giannutri at the turn of the present century, when the agronomist Gualtiero Adami reintroduced the olive and the vine.

I often feel I might like to spend the rest of my days among the Tuscan islands, but for those desiring more than wild nature and happy snorkelling much remains to see. Back on Monte Argentario, follow the Tombolo di Giannella road to the mainland and take the dead straight route across the Albegna valley and up into the hills as far as Manciano. Anyone travelling in this region needs to get used to its pattern of sparse settlement: the sheer inner diversity of Tuscany is brought home to us here, in an area where the spaces between villages can seem either encouraging or alarming according to your mood.

This is poor Tuscany, a far cry from the prosperous farmlands and orchards of the Arno valley or the Chianti. Continually harried by malaria, its towns and hamlets were dismal places when the great reforming Grand Duke Pietro Leopoldo visited them in 1787. In Saturnia, for example, he noted that 'we saw truly terrible faces, discouragement in everybody and no employment', at Sovana 'everything ruined, no walls, weeds growing to the height of a man', at Capalbio and Paganico 'such misery that if no remedy is found, these villages, in a very few years, will no longer exist'.

Exist they do, but their atmosphere is still eloquent of a darker history. The roots of such places are Etruscan, and as in all Etruscan sites a peculiarly haunted, arcane quality clings to the landscape. This in itself is, for me, among the most spectacular in Italy. The few roads lead across grassy plateaux before

---

A rainbow frames Orbetello, seen across its lagoon.

suddenly plunging down into deeply incised river canyons, above which, on beetling plugs of tufa, the various little towns are perched.

Of these the three most memorable lie east of Manciano, along the road leading down towards the Papal frontier and Lake Bolsena. Pitigliano is the first, as it should be for its incomparable position, teetering on the edge of the huge ochre-coloured cliff out of which it has, as it were, organically sprung. Periodically bits of it tumble off, but the town has always picked itself up and gone on again. The Etruscan tomb chambers can be seen hollowed out of the rock as you switchback upwards to the main gate, built, like the crenellated palace in the square beyond, by the Orsini family to whom the whole area belonged during the later Middle Ages. The palace itself now contains municipal offices, but it is worth climbing the courtyard ramp to look at the elegant well-head and the early renaissance portico beyond.

A walk through Pitigliano reveals a typical south Tuscan feature, houses whose upper floors are reached by an outside staircase. The colours are prevailingly sombre, and there is a grizzled, hard-nosed atmosphere of determined survival about the place which is not without appeal. This is especially marked in the Jewish synagogue on the northern wall of the town, ready almost to drop into the gorge below, which it recently threatened to do. That a Jewish community fetched up in so obvious a backwater may seem strange, but the protection of the Grand Duchy, which gained control of Pitigliano in 1604, always extended to Jews. Refugees from persecution in the Papal States, they found a haven here and for two centuries the community, some five or six thousand, maintained a school, a library and a kosher bakery which can still be

Etruscan Pitigliano perches on top of high tufa cliffs.

seen in the Vicolo Margherita. As for the butcher's shop, its meat was so popular that gentiles bought it too, and an atmosphere of almost unprecedented mutual trust and friendship grew up between the two peoples, broken only by a terrible burst of anti-semitism in 1799, during protests against French occupation. There are still a few Jews left in the town and the synagogue has recently been restored.

Pitigliano was the birthplace, in 1702, of one of the most enchanting of eighteenth-century landscape painters, Francesco Zuccarelli. Since he worked mostly in Venice he is always thought of as belonging to the Veneto, but the shaggy bushes and jagged escarpments in his canvases are surely a memory of a southern Tuscan childhood. There is plenty of such atmosphere along the eastward road to Sorano, most obviously

A stone scutcheon at Sorano.

This renaissance lion guards the gateway to the _rocca_ at Pitigliano.

workaday of the three towns, but as impressive in what modern jargon calls its 'overview' as Pitigliano. Slung out along a high spur above the Lente river, it is pinned down at either end by two immense fortresses. The earlier, to the south, is the Fortezza Orsini, built on medieval foundations by the Sienese architect Anton Maria Lari in 1552 and traditionally never taken by besiegers. To the north is the strikingly graceless Masso Leopoldino, built by the last Grand Duke, though local historians seem reluctant to say why.

If Sorano seems somewhat gloomier than its neighbours this is only because of its pronouncedly concave layout. The charm of its old stones and washing-garlanded alleys is no less, and the views into the valley are just as dramatic. There was a small Jewish colony here too, though the synagogue, in the Via del Ghetto, is now a china shop.

Crossing the gorge and taking the westward road brings you to Sovana, one of the loveliest of the Tuscan *borghi*, too small for a town, too grand for a village, a place which, if history had taken other directions, might have become one of the greatest cities in Italy, but is perhaps more attractive in its failure to do so. Hidden on top of its tufa plug amid thick woods, Sovana began as the Etruscan Suana, which became a focal point for commercial and military activity during the sixth century BC. One relic of this period is the vast necropolis of rock-cut tombs, some with sculptures and inscriptions, girdling the cliffs below the town. Sovana's significance increased under the Romans and it remained a valued place of refuge during the barbarian invasions. Hotly contested by various powers in the early Middle Ages, it became a county under the domination of several Roman feudal clans: Orsini, Caetani, Aldobrandeschi. One of the latter, Ildebrando, born here in 1027, is better known as Gregory VII, perhaps the greatest of the medieval popes.

By the sixteenth century all Sovana's splendour was gone, eroded by warfare, economic mismanagement and the growing scourge of malaria. The Medici tried to repopulate it, first with Albanians, then with Greeks from the Mani in the southern Peloponnese, and these unsuccessful efforts were repeated in the eighteenth century when the Hapsburg Grand Dukes hopefully introduced settlers from Lorraine. It was then, and it remains, a barely inhabited ruin.

Standing in the open space (it can scarcely be called a piazza) outside the postcard shop and restaurant is a suitably demoralizing experience. To the left, where are the glories of the Palazzo Comunale, symbol of Sovana's brief independence at the turn of the thirteenth century? Where are the Bourbon del Monte family, who tacked a palace on to the humble loggia built in 1572? To the right of this stands the ruined church of San Mamiliano and, on the other side, Santa Maria has the sort of unadorned intimacy which seems closely in touch with the early medieval spirit and which, in a more prosperous community than Sovana, would have disappeared long ago. The high altar stands beneath a ciborium, a sort of pavilion or baldacchino of decorated marble, venerably antique and probably dating from the eighth century. Against the plain walls patches of decayed fresco stand out, including an absorbing stylistic contrast between the very staid, old-fangled *Madonna with Saints Barbara and Lucy* by the anonymous 'painter of Montemerano', dated 1508, and its neighbour, in a far more sophisticated high renaissance manner, a *Crucifixion* with a Signorellian landscape and clouds, author unknown, painted only ten years later.

The jewel of Sovana, and one of the most potently authentic survivals from the Middle Ages, is the cathedral, standing a little aloof from the town at the end of a street leading past the austere-looking palace where Gregory VII was born. Embowered among olive and cypress with the fields beyond, this church is the more attractive because there has never been any attempt to homogenize its maze of romanesque additions to the fabric and design. The generous apsidal conch, for example, incorporates several of those grotesque corbels and dragon plaques which relate this architecture to a northern world of Celtic and Germanic paganism. We seem to see fogs and forests bristling with 'loathly worms' and gold-guarding monsters, and to hear echoes from far-away Durham, Kilpeck and Lindisfarne sounding in the patterns and figure-sculpture of Sovana's nave capitals, with their biblical scenes and animal masks.

The plainness and purity of this interior, where the falls of sunlight from the clerestory windows intensify the warmth of pinkish-yellow stone, may not rival Sant' Antimo (see p. 151) for grandeur but surely match it for beauty. In the south aisle a travertine urn holds the bones of St Mamilianus, bringer of Christianity to

The stone canopy over the high altar of Santa Maria at Sovana is a precious example of pre-romanesque sculpture.

Sovana, with his delicately carved effigy in bishop's robes by an anonymous renaissance hand. The few paintings, with the exception of Domenico Manetti's bold stab at the Guido Reni manner in his *Martyrdom of St Peter* (1671) on the west wall, are unremarkable. Yet they and the wooden baroque angels in the porch seem pleasantly to share in the overall sense that one day soon this cathedral, already looking impossibly ancient in experience and wisdom, will shrug its stone shoulders and amble off into the countryside, never to be seen again.

From Sovana you cross a broad upland plain, dotted with single oak trees and the occasional farm, a landscape incongruously reminiscent of the Worcestershire where I grew up. North of San Martino sul Fiora, the ground begins to rise gently towards the lower slopes of Monte Amiata, the highest mountain in Tuscany and a geographical constant dominating the entire southern half of the province. Its sharply delineated cone is snow-covered for much of the winter and a favourite haunt of weekend skiers, but elsewhere borax is mined and the thick woodlands of beech, chestnut and fir shelter edible fungi which flavour the local cooking.

The towns and villages clustered round the mountain have a distinctive sense of belonging to it, yet there is a decided ambiguity in the way they manage to evoke the modest plainness of the Maremma while simultaneously hinting at the prosperity of the Sienese farmlands further north. Nowhere is this better exemplified than at Santa Fiora, comfortably tucked into Amiata's south-west shoulder. Until the abolition of feudal lordships in 1789 the little town was an independent county, belonging to a branch of the Sforza family, who rebuilt the medieval castle standing at its centre. Somewhat curiously the building's arcaded ground floor acts as a kind of passageway into a long, narrow piazza with an extremely vigorous open market at one end on weekdays. The houses and churches hint at a certain stateliness, but the oddest indication of modestly continuing prosperity is the *peschiera*, or civic fishpond, at the foot of the hill below the church of Sant'Agostino. Established during the eighteenth century, this harnesses the limpid waters of the River Fiora via a system of streamlets flowing through a pleasing little park into the central pool, well stocked with trout ready for eating by the townsfolk, though who fishes them out and when I could never discover. Were there others like it in Tuscany, or was it always as unique as it seems nowadays?

Monte Amiata's shaggy slopes viewed from Castiglione d'Orcia.

South of Santa Fiora, on the edge of Monte Calvo, Bosio Sforza founded the convent of Selva in 1508. The early nineteenth-century church has one exceptional picture, recently restored after damage to its upper edges. Here the Virgin sits amid musical angels and St John is depicted between the craggy-faced St Jerome and St Francis, with ships on a distant sea. This beautiful *Assumption* is the work of Girolamo di Benvenuto (1470–1524), one of the last great Sienese masters.

Here you can choose whether to circle the mountain by east or west. The eastward road from Santa Fiora will take you to Piancastagnaio, another feudal *borgo* whose machicolated fort was built by the Aldobrandeschi to keep off the forces of the greedy abbot of neighbouring San Salvatore. Grandeur of more peaceable intent marks the nearby Palazzo Bourbon del Monte, by Valentino Martelli (1550–1630), a Perugian architect clearly influenced by Roman models. The churches here cater for every visual taste: medievalists will enjoy Nanni di Pietro's Umbrian gothic frescoes in the Madonna delle Grazie, while those who, like me, have a perverse fondness for artistic byways, can visit the Carmelite sanctuary of the Madonna di San Pietro, where the local master Francesco Nasini, in 1640, carried out an entire sequence of allegorical altarpieces and wall paintings; provincial, yes, but irresistibly exuberant.

Piancastagnaio means 'plain of the chestnut tree' and though chestnuts flourish in various corners of Tuscany – in the Garfagnana, for instance, it often seems as though there is scant chance for any other tree – the particular volcanic geology of Monte Amiata favours some magnificent stands along the road to Abbadia San Salvatore. The abbey itself was founded by Ratchis, King of the Longobards, Italy's Germanic rulers during the early Middle Ages. Deemed far too conciliatory towards the Pope, he was pushed from his throne by the ambitious usurper Astolf after a reign of only four years and compelled to enter the monastery he had established here after having a vision of the Saviour in a pine tree during a hunting trip. Suppressed in 1783, the abbey was only restored to the Benedictines in 1939. Restoration has exposed the romanesque plan of the existing building, mostly of the early eleventh century, with a broad ambo and a crypt whose columns are always said to have come from Ratchis's original church. The king's vision itself forms part of a lively fresco sequence in the presbytery by Francesco Nasini.

Turn left at La Madonna and follow the minor road over the mountain to Arcidosso, heaped up high around an Aldobrandeschi castle and something of a little metropolis for the *amiatesi*. The town produced two figures essentially typical of this rugged region, where the inhabitants staved off hunger with a mainly chestnut-based diet and sought work amid the gruelling conditions of the mercury and borax mines. The first was the shepherd poet Giandomenico Peri (1564–1639), one of the greatest improvisers of his day, who refused to abandon his humble goatskin jacket and leggings even when lured to Florence to perform before the Grand Duke. Otherwise, apart from a disastrous foray into fashionable Rome, where duchesses and cardinals cooed and giggled over his sweetly countrified ways, he never left Amiata.

The other was a more bizarre character altogether, one belonging inalienably to this landscape of shaggy heathlands and bald mountain slopes, the nineteenth-century folk evangelist Davide Lazzaretti, 'the carter saint'. A drunken, wenching blasphemer, who learned to read during valiant service against the Papal army in the Marches, he received a series of divine visions, telling him to change his life and lead men to

The stark open ploughlands of the far south of Tuscany.

redemption. A visit to Pope Pius IX, whose fastidious aristocratic agonizings probably made him rather envious of Davide's uncomplicated faith, was a failure, but the evangelist soon attracted popular support through his evident saintliness. During the early 1870s Davide and his followers, the *giurisdavidici*, established a religious commune on the slopes of Monte Labbro, west of Santa Fiora, attracting some eighty families and the immediate suspicion of the authorities. Church and state combined to crush the subversive heretic as he led a procession up the mountainside to celebrate the feast of the Assumption: ordered by the police to turn back, he refused, and after their rifles had miraculously failed to go off, an infuriated officer placed a pistol against Davide's head and shot him dead. Refused burial at Arcidosso, he lies in the Santa Fiora cemetery and his modern adherents are reduced to a pathetic remnant.

Leaving Arcidosso, turn westwards towards Cinigiano and Sasso d'Ombrone. Here you cross the broad Ombrone itself and follow a dullish stretch of road to Paganico, partly enclosed within the old walls against which so many desperate sieges were made, but which only yielded to a truly devastating conquest in 1555, when the infuriated forces of Cosimo de' Medici massacred the inhabitants and burned the town. For years afterwards the Sienese contemptuously described those down on their luck as 'born among the bushes of Paganico'. Among the treasures not destroyed by Cosimo were the apsidal frescoes in the *parrochiale*, probably the work of Bartolo di Fredi.

Ruins in this part of Italy are so uncommon – and ruined abbeys especially – that San Galgano to the north-west along the winding road from Roccastrada simply has to be seen, and in any case its forlorn

---

Cypress trees mark the essential accents in the Tuscan landscape.

solitude makes it one of Tuscany's most memorable buildings. The great thirteenth-century gothic nave and transepts, with tall pillars and rose windows, are like the splendid carcass of a dead elephant, whose power and beauty are indestructible even in this sort of arrested decay. The abbey was founded in honour of Galgano Guidotti, a young knight who became a hermit on nearby Monte Siepi and was canonized in 1185. It was the Cistercian Order, with their eagerness to settle in the remotest of spots, who built what is essentially an essay in Burgundian gothic in the heart of Tuscany. The remains of the conventual buildings include a refectory with a vaulted ceiling, a chapter-house and a stretch of cloister. At the top of Monte Siepi itself, San Galgano's little hermitage church contains an outstandingly good frescoed *Madonna and Child* with an adoring Eve, from the hand of Ambrogio Lorenzetti.

From San Galgano, return to the main road and strike eastwards from Monticiano to the Siena-Grosseto road. This busy artery is best left as soon as you can, so take the turning right a little to the north, a secondary road running across a delightful expanse of hilltop which becomes wonderfully minor as soon as you get to Murlo. Keep on southwards until you reach the turn to Montalcino.

Bon-viveurs will know this as the home of one of Italy's most highly regarded vintages, the Brunello di Montalcino, which, with its brother wine Rosso di Montalcino (the difference is in the ageing process) was being drunk in England in the reign of Charles II, when it was called Mont-Alchin. That this is also the honeypot of Tuscany is rather less well known, but there are clusters of beehives among the vineyards covering the slopes below the town. You scarcely need such persuasions to climb the hill: Montalcino embodies the perfect Italian synthesis between man and landscape. The lichen-encrusted red tiles, the pinkish stone, the pale yellow and cream washes on

stuccoed walls grow from the surrounding cornfields of the *contado* and, as it were, return to them. There is nothing here of the angry rigidity of the town planner or the development expert, even though Montalcino, in its human dimension, is a prosperous modern community with a goodly measure of civic pride.

Montalcino was Sienese from the day of the crucial battle of Montaperti (1260), and was a haven for refugees from the siege of Siena in 1555. Declaring '*Ubi cives, ibi patria*' ('wherever the city, there the motherland'), these exiles kept up 'the Republic of Siena in Montalcino' as a miserable remnant of former glory under the protection of the French commander Blaise de Montluc, until forced to surrender to Cosimo I in 1559.

In the little Piazza del Popolo at the centre of the town an open-air drama festival is given each year, and the daytime visitor is treated to the bizarre spectacle of that evening's *mise-en-scène* set up ready with the citizens of Montalcino going about their lawful errands on either side. The Palazzo dei Priori at the western end of the square, built at the turn of the fourteenth century, has a tower which unusually combines stone in the lower storeys with brick in the upper. In Piazza Garibaldi behind the palace the old church of Sant'Egidio brings together touches of romanesque and Sienese gothic.

Walk up the hill past Sant'Agostino and turn right towards the pleasantly theatrical neo-classical *duomo*, built in 1818–32 by an architect with the marvellous name of Agostino Fantastici. This is a lovely, airy crest to the town, with fine prospects south towards Monte Amiata and north across the Arbia valley.

Now go down Via Ricasoli, where the old diocesan seminary half-way along has been turned into an excellent municipal gallery. Some of the best exhibits are those marvellous polychrome wooden statues of angels and saints whose speechless eloquence of gesture and expression makes them among the most potent creations of the Middle Ages. But there are good pictures too, including an *Adoration* by Girolamo di Benvenuto, with a gorgeous stretch of distant blue mountains for a background, and Bartolo di Fredi's *Coronation of the Virgin*, with particularly graceful angel musicians, an organist and a viol player.

From here, past shops selling honey and beeswax and lavender, you reach the grand fourteenth-century *rocca*, the work of Mino Foresi and Domenico di Feo, with a Medici bastion tacked on in 1570 by Baldassare Lanci. This has now been most agreeably converted into a showcase for the good things of Montalcino's earth, Brunello and other wines, cheeses, oil, dried mushrooms and magnificent local hams and sausages. There can be few more agreeable ways of rounding off a morning than a taste and a sip of what lunch may have to offer, in the shade of medieval towers.

Take the road down the hill behind the fortress in the direction of Sant'Antimo. Here in the valley stands another of those great Tuscan abbeys, some may feel the most beautiful of all. Sant'Antimo was said to have been established by Charlemagne, and its Benedictine foundation certainly dates from the early ninth century. The fact that the church survives in its present form, as a perfect example of the finest romanesque design, doubtless reflects the monastery's early decline, from the thirteenth century onwards.

The use of travertine, that most attractive of materials, gives the entire building a gentle warmth like that of an animal's skin. On the façade of the west end you can see the name of the architect, Azzone dei Porcari, who gave the church its stocky bell-tower and incorporated decorative features from an earlier structure on the site. Inside, the alabaster capitals of the nave lead up to an altar whose Latin inscription

The seventeenth-century pilgrimage church of the Madonna di Soccorso, Montalcino.

details the founding of the church: in the crypt below, the altar is actually a Roman tomb dating from AD 347. The ambulatory behind the tomb, giving on to three little apsidal chapels, betrays the French influence which ensured that this feature survived in the design of cathedrals and abbeys of the gothic period. You can climb up to the triforium by a spiral staircase in the wall.

From Sant'Antimo, take the road on to the edge of Monte Amiata and then turn north towards Castiglione d'Orcia, a fortified *borgo* of the Aldobrandeschi before it passed to Siena in 1250. This, and its neighbouring Rocca d'Orcia, just across the way as it were, have no special distinctions, but the weathering of age has given them a singular charm. Castiglione, what is more, has a Pietro Lorenzetti *Madonna and Child* in the church of SS Stefano e Degna, whose composition is among the most harmonious of any medieval painting I know. The same subject is portrayed by Giovanni di Paolo in Rocca's San Simeone, with a vigorously Tuscan *bambino* at his mother's exposed breast. The *rocca* itself is a huge polygonal tower heaped up on the hilltop, the work of the Sienese Salimbeni family, who gained control here in 1368.

On the way north towards San Quirico d'Orcia you may pause to take a bath at the ancient spa of Bagno Vignoni, where the hot springs bubble up in the main square of the village. The cure, for 'traumatic illness', chlorosis and fistula among other things, has been going since Roman times. Lorenzo de' Medici failed to find relief for his arthritis here, Montaigne called the place 'a flea pit', but an admiring tribute was paid by a sixteenth-century member of the Sienese Tolomei family. The Greek epigram which he had inscribed on one of the pillars of the portico round the main bath addresses 'you Naiads who spread fire through the waters'. It was St Catherine of Siena who made the most original use of the waters by tormenting her flesh with the heat. A local tradition calls the white streaks which occasionally appear in the water *la strada di Santa Caterina* (St Catherine's highway).

San Quirico itself is approached by a sweep of road over a bridge, positively made for carriages to bowl across. Rebuilt by Maestro Antonio Lombardo in 1472, its machicolated walls faced a host of sieges, worst of which was probably that of Cesare Borgia in 1502. When he finally took the town, it was deserted save for two ancient men and nine old women. Believing they knew where the civic coffers were hidden, he roasted them all over slow fires, but since they could or would not tell him anything, he had them done to a frazzle and then vented his rage on the empty houses.

The patron saint Quiricus was the son of Julita, a noblewoman of Iconium in Asia Minor, who resisted the governor's attempts to convert her to paganism during Diocletian's third-century persecutions. Her little baby, whom she held on her knee, lisped 'I too am a Christian' and scratched the governor's face. The end of the story may be imagined. Mother and child are commemorated on 16 June every year.

The Collegiata church dedicated to these martyrs is of exceptional architectural interest, partly because of the varied pitch of its roofs and partly because of its three fine late romanesque doorways. The westernmost of these has columns resting on the backs of crouching lions and bound together by serpentine knots, while the south portal, with two figures in tunics and buskins on far more recognizably leonine beasts, is probably the work of Giovanni Pisano.

There are lions inside as well. On the floor of the nave is a relief sculpture of Count Heinrich of Nassau, who died of malaria here on his way back from the Roman Jubilee of 1450. He is shown in the full armour of a knight, with his head on a cushion. The lion at his

San Quirico d'Orcia retains its medieval walls and gateways.

feet is the badge of his family. In the chapel to the left nobody should ignore one of Sano di Pietro's most attractive works, an altarpiece complete with predella panels and lunette scenes of the Resurrection, rich in reds and golds, with little donors tucked in like felicitous afterthoughts below.

The 1725 baroque choir and altar are complemented by an organ made in Cortona during the same period. Lavish in gilded garlands, this instrument was originally intended for Monte Oliveto. Truly astounding here, however, is the set of inlaid wooden choir-stalls by the Sienese master Antonio Barili (1453–1516), who finished them in 1502. Barili's perception of his subjects is not at all Tuscan in feeling, but much more like similar work in Venice, where Carpaccio and Antonello were busy surrounding the fugitive moment in little breezes of realism. A spray of fruit with a perching goldfinch bursts in across an arch with a prospect of a distant garden. A bearded man holds back a shutter. Another, in a furred cap, turns his head to listen to an organ which nobody is playing. The doors of a cupboard swing open to reveal a carpenter's tool-kit.

In the choir is an energetically carved marble monument to a periwigged member of the Chigi family, who lived in the old palace south-east of the church. Designed by Felice del Lino in 1679 for the nephew of Pope Alexander VII, the building is now in a miserably ramshackle state, the more regrettable because of its wealth of baroque fresco work. A contemporary document indicates the painters by their Christian names and specialities – 'Giovanni Battista of the figures, Francesco of the landscapes, Girolamo of the perspectives, Camillo of the ornaments' – but since the state and the Chigi have reached an impasse, the whole thing is on the verge of collapse.

Further along the street is San Quirico's 'particular', not reproduced, as far as I know, anywhere else in Tuscany, and remarkable in any case within the context of its period. This is the Orti Leonini, a large triangular plot of terraced gardens, laid out by Diomede Leoni in 1535 on waste ground within the town walls and, though until recently private property, always enjoyed by citizens taking an evening promenade. Compartments edged by clipped box hedge and ilex walks surround a statue by Giuseppe Mazzuoli of Cosimo III in Roman dress, and even if the whole affair is now a trifle scruffy it is a good place for a quiet pre-prandial stroll.

East from San Quirico lies Pienza. If it were not so overwhelmingly attractive this would be a very sad place indeed because it is nothing less than a monument to unfulfilled ambition. Europe is littered with planned and planted towns, which their founders intended as glorious memorials to their foresight and benevolence. Some, like Berlin or the Pest section of Budapest, have become major capital cities, but many others, like the settlements in the Welsh Marches established by the all-powerful Mortimer family and nowadays mere lumps in the ground, are simply the graveyards of departed hopes.

In turning his native village of Corsignano into a stately town to be called Pienza in his honour, Pope Pius II was living up to the meaning of his name. As Aeneas Sylvius Piccolomini, he had been born here in 1405 and it was an act of family piety, as much as anything else, to make poor little 'Corsignano of the robbers' into a symbol of the loftiest renaissance values. The architect Bernardo Rossellino, under the tutelage of the enormously influential Leon Battista Alberti (1404–72), was commissioned to build a cathedral, a papal palace and a town hall, and the various cardinals were bidden to erect handsome

A restored medieval fresco crowns the Porta al Murello, Pienza.

The delightfully simple cloister of San Francesco at Pienza.

A corner of the fifteenth-century cathedral at Pienza.

dwellings for themselves on pain of losing important privileges.

Alas, the initiative, bravely begun, came to nothing. By the time the major public works around the central square, now named Piazza Pio II, were completed and a few cardinals had started to build, Pius himself was dead, and the princes of the church, leaving off with a sigh of relief, returned to Rome, abandoning Pienza to slumber amid its olive groves. The result is a quite incongruously splendid village, in which the noblest architectural concepts mingle with the homely plainness of peasant cottages overlooking some of the most attractive open countryside in Tuscany.

The 'intellectual daylight' of humanism is nowhere seen to better advantage than in the cathedral, which Rossellino executed between 1459 and 1462, with

considerable misgivings as to Pius's chosen site on the edge of a slippery slope (giving problems which were surmounted only with the huge projecting bulwarks sustaining the presbytery). The patterns of the façade play skilfully with the contrasting heights of the arches and varying forms of the pediments, but nothing quite prepares us for the singularity of the interior. Pius wanted, and got, a *domus vitrea*, a house of glass, into which natural light flowed freely through a series of tall windows. Ironically, for this most Catholic of popes, the resulting effect is overwhelm-

The harmonious façade of the cathedral at Pienza was designed by Bernardo Rossellino in 1459.

ingly Protestant. The Reformation and the plain glazing of Dutch and English churches suddenly seem very close, even as the groping darkness of buildings such as San Giovanni Forisportam at Pistoia appears light years away.

As a consequence the pictures here can actually be seen, without any need to peer through candle flames or fumble for switches, and exceptionally fine they are. All five were commissioned by the Pope from outstanding Sienese masters of the day – a *Virgin and Child with Saints* by Giovanni di Paolo (1403–82), in which purple and blue are the dominant colours, the same theme treated in a more patently old-fashioned vein by Sano di Pietro, two distinctly contrasting altarpieces by Matteo di Giovanni, with an agonizingly vigorous *Flagellation* in one of the lunettes, and an opulent *Assumption of the Virgin*, between dignified pairs of conversing saints, the work of Lorenzo di Pietro, always known as Vecchietta (1412–80).

There is yet more superlative art in the Canonica, the former palace of the cathedral canons, opposite the door from the crypt, including a marvellous portable triptych by the Osservanza Master and a luridly colourful *Madonna della Misericordia* by Bartolo di Fredi, though perhaps the most remarkable exhibit of all is the richly worked cope presented by the Byzantine Greek Thomas Palaeologus to Pope Pius. This is in the style known as Opus Anglicanum, which carried the fame of English embroiderers and weavers across late medieval Europe. Pius's crozier and mitre lie nearby.

Opposite the Canonica is his palace, still occupied until very recently by the Piccolomini family after whom it is named, part of whose collection you can see displayed on the first floor. Rossellino excelled himself here in the three-tiered loggia looking over the garden and in the Corinthian grace of the courtyard arcades. Compare this with Rodrigo Borgia's mean-spirited palace opposite, in which the wily cardinal, who became Pius's successor as Pope Alexander VI, simply classicized an existing piece of gothic, shown clearly in the masonry above the first floor windows.

With its sleepy cats, its geraniums in pots and its *pecorino* cheese, I find Pienza a joy to amble around and not at all the mournful, moralizing spot it might so easily be. Pius II might not have been as successful as he desired in his eternally restless life, but there are many worse monuments than this lovely and surprising place, in which 'the middle of nowhere' suddenly achieves a radiant significance.

The courtyard of Palazzo Piccolomini at Pienza was designed by Bernardo Rossellino.

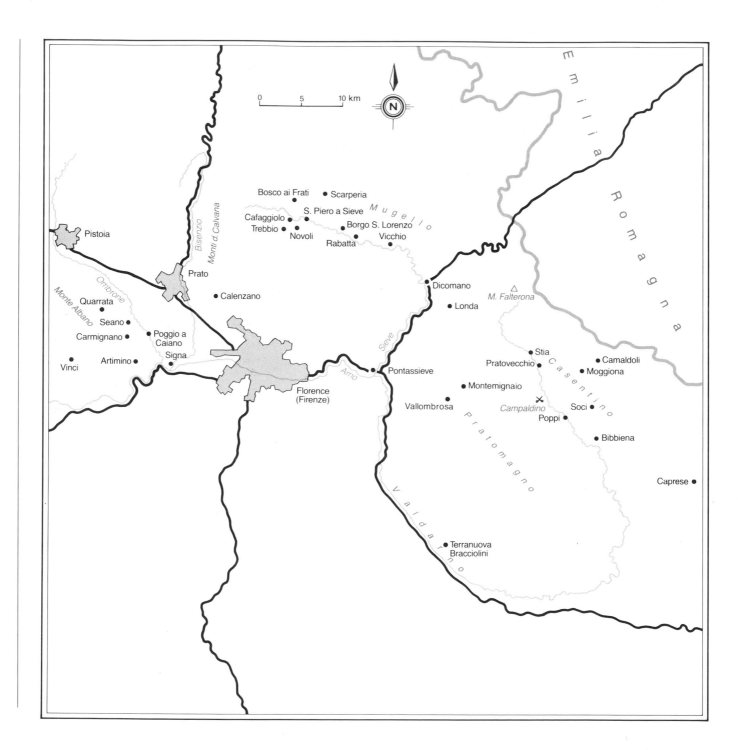

5
Prato, Pistoia and the North-East

Signa – Pistoia – Prato – the Mugello – Scarperia –
Borgo San Lorenzo – Dicomano – Stia – Poppi –
Soci – Bibbiena – Vallombrosa

Westward out of Florence, hugging the Arno along the Empoli road, you enter one of the most exuberantly fertile regions of Tuscany. This is the kind of landscape the old guidebook writers always used to describe as 'smiling', its hillsides festooned with vines or the pale greyish-green of olives, and yellow villas scattered along the ridges of each steeply plunging valley. Not so long ago, if the family were not in residence, a friendly *fattore* or *fattoressa* might be persuaded to show you the garden or even the villa itself: nowadays the cypress avenues, their serried trees stuck up like rows of daggers, are more likely to end in an angry flourish of burglar alarms, slavering Rottweilers and notices proclaiming '*proprietà privata*'.

Perhaps this is not so very different from the atmosphere in which most of these houses were originally conceived. Tranquil and harmonious as they appear, the very epitome of sophisticated rustic idleness, the presence of a central tower and the occasional half-humorous band of crenellation along the parapet are reminders that many of them began as miniature strongholds in the bad old days of Guelph and Ghibelline, when every hilltop was a potential lookout post for the glint of approaching weapons.

Even under the stable rule of the Medici, a sense of the villa as a potential fortress was seldom altogether relinquished. Artimino, reached by crossing the river and turning left at Signa, is a case in point. There was already an established game preserve here, created by Duke Cosimo, by the time his grandson Ferdinand I commissioned Bernardo Buontalenti (1536–1608) to build him a country retreat in 1594. The emphasis was on simplicity and the design has little of the obvious appeal to elegance or charm found elsewhere among Medici villas. The four flanking towers stand out like bastions, and the functional plainness of the façades is echoed by the interior, most notable for Justus Utens's splendid series of prospects of all the grand-ducal properties, decorating the lunettes of the grand saloon on the first floor.

Each is a precise portrayal of a house and its surrounding park, with the landscape stretching into blueish vagueness beyond. The quasi-aerial view and the little figures of horsemen and carriages giving scale to the foreground are evident ancestors of Johann Kipp's detailed engravings of English country houses published a century later, but then the whole nature of Tuscan renaissance *villeggiatura* has had a far stronger influence on the lifestyles of rural Britain than is sometimes supposed.

Left **Bernardo Buontalenti designed the handsome staircase and loggia of Villa Medici at Artimino.**

Above **Hardly bigger than a parish church, the priory of San Lorenzo is near Montelupo.**

163

After Ferdinand, who used Artimino as a summer headquarters from which to administer all his other estates, few of the Medici seem ever to have cared for the place, though that delightfully engaging figure Francesco Redi recommended dismal podgy Cosimo III to take some weight-reducing exercise in the park. Nowadays the villa opens on Wednesdays and sells its own wine.

The essential Medici villa, however, and the prototype of every country house ever built since the Renaissance, lies to the north-east, on the main Pistoia road at Poggio a Caiano. Here, above the River Ombrone and looking across the flat vale of the Arno towards the scatter of suburban Florence with Brunelleschi's dome as a distant eyecatcher, stands the first modern statement of the idea that the country might actually provide a serene refuge as opposed to a lawless wilderness. Completed in 1474 to the designs of Giuliano da Sangallo, the villa of Poggio a Caiano enshrines all those hankerings for the famous country houses of antiquity – Horace's Sabine farm, Cicero at Tusculum or Hadrian at Tivoli – which typified its creator, Lorenzo de' Medici. Italian architecture has few buildings more handsome in finish, more relaxed and confident in execution or more refreshing to the eye in its synthesis of colours, textures and lines.

Lorenzo bought the property from a fellow Florentine, Giovanni Rucellai, and set about the immediate creation of a work designed to express the dignity and grandeur of neo-platonic aspirations, a perfect setting for a poetic declamation by Angelo Poliziano or a philosophical discourse by Marsilio Ficino, both Lorenzo's contemporaries. The concept of a fortress-villa, clustering towers around a central courtyard, was set aside in favour of a plan as original as it was attractive. Guests were confronted with a colonnaded central portico under a pediment framing the Medici arms, above a brick arcade running the length of the building.

The message, defiant in its sobriety of expression, is obvious. Let others struggle and kill, for we have better matters in hand. As if to reinforce this, Andrea Sansovino's frieze of blue and white terracotta tiles carries a series of reliefs symbolizing Lorenzo's good government, its chaste classicism for all the world like something from a later age, of Wedgwood, Flaxman and the 'Ode on a Grecian Urn'.

Later generations cherished the spirit of a villa which the Emperor Charles V, much given to airing his views on art, pronounced 'not a suitable building for a private citizen'. For the walls of the great barrel-vaulted *salone*, judged by Vasari to be the most beautiful in the world, Lorenzo's son Pope Leo X commissioned frescoes from three of the best sixteenth-century Florentine hands. Andrea del Sarto (1486–1531) contributed an idiosyncratic *Caesar Receiving Egyptian Tribute*, a symphony in attitudes and gestures (the giraffe in the distance was a gift to Lorenzo from the Mameluke Sultan of Egypt). Franciabigio (1482–1525) played the antiquarian in his *Triumph of Cicero*, alluding to Cosimo de' Medici's return from exile, and Pontormo portrayed the Roman garden deities Vertumnus and Pomona as a peasant boy and girl lolling on a sunlit wall. Later in the century Alessandro Allori took up the Medicean theme in two luminously colourful episodes from Livy, painted for Grand Duke Francesco, who spent long periods here in the company of his mistress Bianca Cappello.

Bianca's story was so typical of late renaissance Italy that it grabbed the imagination of dramatists and poets from the outset. Shakespeare's contemporary Thomas Middleton made her the heroine of his *Women Beware Women*, and Browning romanticized her meeting with

Tuscany is full of unexpected cameos like this.

Francesco in *The Statue and the Bust*. Daughter of a patrician family, she eloped from her native Venice to Florence with a youth whom she promptly abandoned for the favours of the Grand Duke. The Venetian Republic, having originally blackened her name, hastened to acknowledge 'a faithful daughter of Saint Mark', but her triumph was momentary. The Grand Duchess banished her from the city, and when she at last became Francesco's wife she had to endure the mortification of being shunned by the Florentine nobility and seeing her son excluded from the succession with the damning label of '*figlio supposto*'.

Her apartment, with its magnificent chimneypiece and a curious little staircase to her bedchamber, witnessed a short-lived happiness. Bianca died within a few hours of the Duke she loved, on 19 October 1587, both of them poisoned, it was instantly rumoured, with an envenomed pie, though the cause is more likely to have been a severe virus infection. The imprint of her presence is matched by equally powerful memories of other owners: Elisa Baciocchi, Napoleon's sister, who presented the operas of Paisiello and Spontini in the enchanting little neo-classical theatre, his wife the Empress Marie Louise, whose architect Pasquale Poccianti designed the sinuously elegant flanking staircases on the main façade, and the famous 'bella Rosina', Countess of Mirafiori, morganatic wife of Victor Emmanuel II, first king of Italy (their beds are flounced and valanced in masculine blue and feminine pink). Even the garden, a synthesis of Italian formalism with the English wilderness manner, has its place in horticultural history.

Pontormo's surviving works are few enough, so after enjoying Vertumnus and Pomona, you may choose to take the road south-west to Carmignano, where the parish church of San Michele contains his undoubted masterpiece, the great *Visitation* of 1530. In his own day Pontormo, whose baptismal name was

Jacopo Carrucci, was considered decidedly odd, and a glance at a diary he kept during the 1550s bears out the picture of a reclusive hypochondriac. Nearly all the entries concern the state of his health, what he ate and the details of current work. On 15 March 1555, for example, he drew an arm in his *Ascension of Souls* and had fish, cheese, figs, nuts and eleven ounces of bread: a day or two later, feeling fragile owing to the bad weather, he took to his bed and dined off poached fish and greens. And so forth. He seems to have had few friends, apart from the equally talented Agnolo Bronzino, and practically never to have left his house.

The haunted quality of his paintings has perhaps been overrated. Anyone contemplating his *Deposition* and *Annunciation* in the Capponi chapel at Santa Felicita in Florence is likely to be not so much disturbed as transported into a world of buoyant stillness, in which the mask-like eyes and profiles of the figures seem to encase a hermetic silence. Maybe there is more to the diary than poached fish and greens. Certainly the Carmignano *Visitation* suggests so. The figures of the Virgin and St Elizabeth are like a pair of huge insects enmeshed in carapaces of pink and grey, their faces imbued with the gentleness of superior wisdom, a brace of sybilline giantesses whose stature matches their momentous roles in the history of mankind.

Heads still full of Pontormo, set off through the Carmignano vineyards, whose velvety Cabernet red wine offers a more than modest alternative to Chianti or Montepulciano. This is some of my favourite Tuscan countryside, with roads teetering up the switchback slopes to glimpses of red-roofed farms amid the oak woods above swift-plashing rivers. A landscape for seventeenth-century painters, you half expect to catch

Lines of vines snaking across the hills are an essential ingredient of the Tuscan landscape.

a glimpse of Claude Lorrain or Gaspar Dughet, pencil in hand. But a turn to the north at Seano and south again at Quarrata and a few kilometres more of plunges and lurches over the hills will bring you face to face with a greater yet more enigmatic presence than either of these.

Leonardo da Vinci (1452–1519) took his name from the small town where he was baptized, on a spur of Monte Albano, a semicircular hog's-back running from Pistoia down to the Arno. In fact he was born a little to the north, in the hamlet of Anchiano, but the birthplace, restored almost to extinction, is not half so interesting as Vinci itself, perched around the medieval castle which houses a Leonardian museum.

Few of Tuscany's museums are ideally suited to children, easily bored with squares of canvas and lumps of stone, but this is perfect for the notional wet afternoon with the kids, as the constant presence of younger visitors makes clear. The exhibition concentrates exclusively on Leonardo the inventor, that amazing document in tireless ingenuity and unrealized potential. With meticulous attention to detail, and using the most attractive materials, modern Italian craftsmen have reconstructed the wondrous machines for flight, war, industry and entertainment which he devised but was never able to bring to life. The drawing-board, in the shape of pages from his famous notebooks, with their mysterious hooked and barbed script, is revealed in display cases, including one devoted to the well-known bicycle doodle. Was it his invention or merely a jotting by an inspired pupil?

Pondering this, turn northwards across Monte Albano itself, along a road whose eccentric arabesques are more than compensated for by a wealth of grand prospects on either side. The joy of Tuscany lies in the simple fact that so few of its ways are straight, a pleasure to contrast with the inexorable grids and pistes of Lombardy and Emilia Romagna. Only when it slips down on to the plain does the road align itself so as to shoot smoothly over the motorway and into Pistoia.

Home of the pistol and the *pistole*, a coin which became the standard currency of the Spanish empire, Pistoia is a textbook example of the way in which the average Italian city grew, from classical beginnings to renaissance apogee. A glance at the map shows the typical Roman square plan of Pistoria, where Sallust tells us that the rebel Catiline was defeated in 62 BC, spreading outwards to the line of a later girdle of walls dating from the early Middle Ages, marked by the Corso Gramsci and Via dei Baroni. Further still are the surviving ramparts and bastions set up by the Florentines, whose protection Pistoia was forced to seek in 1329, worn out with trying to hold on to its independence.

For a place of its size and historical experience it is one of the least attractive towns in Tuscany. The prevailing colour of its stucco is a sort of sickly yellow, compounded with dust and grime, highlighted by the gloomy greyish brown of stone facings. There is a charmless quality in its streets and a peculiar absence of stateliness, as if, under Florentine domination, it had somehow given up for good.

Yet it deserves a visit for several reasons. Lovers of north Tuscan romanesque, with its exuberant patternings of banded marble, will delight in the churches here, noblest of which is San Giovanni Fuorcivitas, in Via Cavour. Fuorcivitas is *fuori città* – outside the city – which it was when founded in the eighth century, though the present building is a splendid essay in romanesque expansiveness dating from two hundred years later. Since there are hardly any windows and only the weakest of illumination, it is almost impossible to enjoy the pulpit by Nicola Pisano's talented follower Guglielmo da Pisa, but a patch of rather crude lighting does allow you to appreciate the church's real treasure, Luca della Robbia's glazed terracotta *Visitation*. Fresh from the

In Via Sant'Andrea, Pistoia.

food market, spread out around a half-hearted sort of piazza, with butchers' shops, vegetable stalls selling sheaves of those toothsome weeds and grasses which make Italian salads the most satisfying in the world, cheese vendors with their ochreous chunks of *grana* and sallow-hued *pecorino*, and fishmongers with the speckled, gleaming, goggle-eyed spoils of that morning's catch from Livorno.

Beyond this lies what ought to be, but somehow is not, the city's heart. Nearly all the components of the Piazza del Duomo are individually handsome. The elegant gothic baptistery, completed to Andrea Pisano's designs in 1359, boasts fine bas-reliefs of the life of St John the Baptist, and a *Madonna and Child* in a lunette above the porch. Slightly to the right of this, the Palazzo del Podestà has the functional, no-nonsense quality of the best Italian medieval civic architecture, and next to it the *duomo*, with its arcaded façade, the arched campanile and the looming gothic Palazzo del Comune form an exemplary architectural grouping. Yet the square cries out for something in the way of human presence and movement.

Almost as soon as you enter the south aisle of the *duomo* you chance on the tomb of the town's most famous son, the diplomat, teacher and master poet Cino da Pistoia. The friend and admirer of Dante, and a fellow sufferer with him in the age's political upheavals, he is one of the most refined exponents of the *Dolce Stil Novo*, the first great outpouring of Italian vernacular poetry around the turn of the thirteenth century. He died in 1337 and Cellino di Nesi, builder of the baptistery, designed his monument that year. Below the gothic tabernacle, a relief panel shows Cino himself in the act of teaching a class of ardent young pupils, including, it is said, the youthful Boccaccio.

Further along the same aisle is the apsidal chapel of St James, whose massive silver altar, begun in 1287, went on being encrusted, adjusted and added to for the next two centuries to produce what is essentially a

same theme by Pontormo, you can hardly fail to savour the contrast. The intrinsic drama here is in the sobriety of the two white figures, whose simply arranged hair and plainness of dress give them the high seriousness of women in a George Eliot novel – Dorothea's meeting with Rosamund in *Middlemarch* perhaps. There is nothing quite like this elsewhere in Italian art.

Narrow lanes opposite the church run up to the only really engaging corner of central Pistoia. This is the

complete display of the medieval silversmith's art. Two of the figures (there are over six hundred) are by Brunelleschi, but the liveliest work appears in the panels by Andrea di Jacopo d'Ognabene, representing moments from the life of Christ, full of the kind of incidental movement – turning heads, slowly disappearing bodies and eloquent gestures – which give such scenes a singular directness.

While Andrea was working on these panels during the early fourteenth century, the *pistoiesi* were completing their Palazzo del Comune on the eastern side of the square (the black marble head above the central window, representing a Moorish king of Majorca defeated in battle by the Pisans, dates from a hundred years earlier). Among the grandest of Tuscany's civic palaces, it also contains one of the more arresting provincial art galleries, not merely because of a recent rearrangement allowing the pictures to be enjoyed in the context of adequate light and space. This is a collection designed for those of us whose knees start to tremble at yet another bunch of art-historical crusts by uninspired followers of Giotto or Botticelli. The presence of good baroque and eighteenth- and nineteenth-century canvases – look, for example, at Ciccio Napoletano's macabre battle fantasies, Pompeo Batoni's *Madonna of the Rosary* or Emilio Busi's heroic *Austrians driven from Genoa* – and of a series of excellent portraits of the Puccini family (no relation to the composer) is a cordial to palates jaded with 'the enchantments of the Middle Age'.

From here it is worth a step down the lane into the frowzy Via Pacini which leads to the Piazza San Bartolomeo, with its eponymous church. The sculptured portico showing Christ giving commandments to his Apostles under a frieze of lions attacking a dragon makes an absorbing transition from early romanesque to the last burst of the style, shown by Guido da Como's pulpit in the north aisle. Whatever the incidental beauties of the panels, it is the two lions and the prostrate merchant upholding its three columns which give the whole ensemble force and vitality.

At its northern end, Via Pacini debouches into a square in front of the Ospedale del Ceppo, Pistoia's answer to the Florentine foundling hospital of Santa Maria Nuova, under whose tutelage it was placed in the sixteenth century. Pistoia was always throwing ripostes at Florence in one way or another: legend has it, for example, that a monstrous statue used to top the gateway of the *rocca* at Carmignano perpetually caught in the act of making the very rude Italian sign known as 'the fig' in the direction of the hated city. The Ospedale del Ceppo's rivalry is a good deal nobler. In 1514 Leonardo Bonafede, the *spedalingo* or warden, added the portico and initiated its admirable frieze of enamelled terracotta panels, displaying the Seven Works of Mercy and the Cardinal Virtues. The former series, strikingly unidealized and anticipating the bourgeois realism which marks certain aspects of late renaissance Italian art, was carried out by Santi Buglioni and Filippo di Lorenzo Paladini, craftsmen in the circle of Giovanni della Robbia (1469–1529), who himself created the figures of the Virtues in the roundels above. *Ceppo*, incidentally, means 'tree stump', in which the charitable offerings were originally collected.

From Pistoia you have a choice of four roads eastwards to Prato, and if not in a hurry you may choose the northernmost, hugging the Apennine foothills dotted with villas and ruined castles. The main Milan-Rome railway line runs down the valley of the Bisenzio, where generations of foreign travellers had their first glimpse of olive-and-cypress Tuscany, with the *Duomo* of Florence spectrally alluring in the

The *duomo* at Pistoia is flanked by the medieval Palazzo del Podestà.

distance. In a general zeal to reach the city itself, Prato is all too easily overlooked. The cavernous grandeur of its station platforms is inversely proportional to the mere handful of trains which actually stop there, and its rampantly industrial appearance from the motorway and the approach roads is scarcely inviting to drivers in search of the picturesque. Florentines, what is more, make slighting jokes about the *pratesi* and like to give the impression that the town is simply a downmarket outpost of the City of the Lily.

This is a mistake. Not only can Prato challenge Pistoia in its 'monuments and things of worth that do adorn this town', but it is far more handsome and lively than its near neighbour. The streets, squares and cafés are packed with young people – the average age of the *pratesi* often seems to be around 22 – and the agreeable sense of consumer Italy bent on pleasure, adornment and never mind the expense, is everywhere. If I sound a trifle defensive about Prato, it is only from a feeling that no visit to Tuscany is worth anything unless it mingles aesthetic raptures with a willingness to enjoy the modern life which provides their context, and Prato is just the spot in which to do so.

Its citizens have something to be smug about. The great textile industry built up here during the early nineteenth century has made the town into one of Italy's richest, giving rise to the old *canard* that there has never been a decent operatic performance here because the *pratesi* are all deaf from the incessant rattle of a myriad looms (in fact its Teatro Metastasio now offers excellent drama). While the rag trade has brought prosperity, a solid Euro-Communist municipal government, always the upholder of civic virtues in Italy, has ensured an agreeable compromise between mercantile wealth and the survival of the historic centre.

Clothiers and weavers were crucial to the life of Prato from the beginning, most famous of them all

being Francesco di Piero Datini (1330–1410), the 'Merchant of Prato', who gave Iris Origo a title for her magnificent study based on a rummage through his papers. A hundred years before Datini, the wonderfully named Panfollia Dagomari, a powerful Ghibelline of the city, left funds for the building of a great fort designed to protect the imperial highway of his master the Emperor Frederick II. A restless, gifted eccentric, Frederick was one of medieval Italy's most forceful figures, and though his presence can be sensed elsewhere in Tuscany, he belonged more emphatically to the Muslim-orientated world of Apulia and Sicily. His looming, white, battlemented stronghold, the first eyecatcher anyone sees on entering Prato, was begun in 1237 by Apulian architects, and has more obvious affinities with the Crusader castles of the Levant or with the kind of fortress thrown up by his Plantagenet kinsmen to subdue the Welsh than with anything specifically Italian.

West of the Castello dell'Imperatore lie two notable churches, the northernmost of which, Santa Maria delle Carceri, has its niche in architectural history. Built in 1484 by Giuliano da Sangallo to a Greek cruciform plan, it inspired a whole clutch of similar buildings from Rome to Venice, as well as foreshadowing the most original of Sir Christopher Wren's designs for St Paul's Cathedral (ultimately rejected by a stick-in-the-mud dean and chapter). San Francesco, directly opposite the castle, has a typical green and white marble banded façade from the late thirteenth century.

Opening times for both churches are irregular, but try to get a glimpse of Andrea della Robbia's evangelists in the dome of Santa Maria, and Niccolò di Pietro Gerini's frescoes in the chapter-house of San

Francesco Datini, the Merchant of Prato, gazes down on the city he enriched during the late fourteenth century.

PRATO, PISTOIA AND THE NORTH-EAST

Francesco, showing scenes from the lives of St Matthew and St Anthony Abbot.

At the top of teeming Via Cairoli is the Piazza del Comune, with Datini's statue and a little fountain sporting a youthful Bacchus. On the east side of the arcaded square, its bars, banks and shops at the apex of provincial chic, the brick bulk of the Palazzo Pretorio – notice the oddly Venetian cast of its twin-arched windows – houses the Galleria Comunale, which flings together an agreeable mishmash of fair-to-middling medieval and renaissance pictures. Amid a clutch of Neapolitan and Roman *vedute*, and canvases by unfairly neglected Tuscan masters such as Ludovico Cigoli (1559–1613) and Giandomenico Ferretti (1692–1766), the *clou* of the collection is Filippo Lippi's *Nativity*, in which the 'shepherds abiding in the fields' steal the show with their unabashed charm.

Lippi (1406–69), whom Browning was to make such an irresistible poetic mouthpiece for the sanctity of beauty in art, was generous with his talents in Prato, as well he might have been, given his passion for Lucrezia Buti, a young novice at the convent of Santa Margherita. Having used her as a model for the Madonna, he contrived to steal her away, and she became the mother of his son, the equally talented Filippino. Filippo himself never wanted to be a monk, and Browning perfectly expresses his raging sexual itch. Cosimo de' Medici once had him locked in his room to get a picture finished, but he succeeded in climbing out of the window, using the classic knotted sheets device, and thereafter, as Vasari tells us, Cosimo 'was wont to say that artists of genius were to be treated reverently and not as simple hacks'.

His love for his own *métier* emerges in the frescoes decorating the choir of the cathedral, completed, after some dozen years' work, in 1466. The cycle on the right-hand wall shows scenes from the life of John the Baptist, that on the left episodes from the story of St Stephen, each magnificent in its exuberant fusion of Christian and pagan, an obvious attempt to render everything within the context of the antique. It is difficult indeed to think of frescoes from the same period which make such a clear appeal to that sense of the past which the Renaissance was so rapidly evolving. In their intensity of reds and blues, in their architectural fancies and wafts of Orientalism *avant-la-lettre*, these paintings celebrate the much despised principle of art as decoration. No solemn or stuffy response to them will do: Lippi knew all about joy and wanted us to share in it. Praising the grandeur and emotional charge of the work, Vasari asks us to admire the poses and costuming of the figures equally, especially in the famous *Banquet of Herod*, with Lucrezia Buti as a dancing Salome and an assembly of sophisticated Tuscans. He sagely notes that because of Filippo's skill 'the many reprehensible circumstances in his life were passed over without a word'.

It is enough to compare these frescoes with the drearily ugly cycle by Agnolo Gaddi adorning the Chapel of the Holy Girdle in the cathedral's north-west corner. The Girdle of Our Lady was given to St Thomas at the moment of her Assumption into Heaven, as a further challenge to his incredulity, and subsequently brought from Palestine by the merchant Michele Dagomari in a box made of reeds. As a miraculous relic it is shown to the faithful five times each year from Easter to Christmas.

For its exposition a special pulpit was thrown up outside the west door in 1434, designed by Michelozzo with a whirligig relief of dancing cherubs by Donatello. Joy is here too in the extraordinary rhythmic bounce of the chubby-legged, puffy-cheeked children as they stamp and skip around the white marble bowl – though the original, for greater

Donatello's exquisite open-air pulpit in the Piazza del Duomo, Prato.

safety, is in the little cathedral museum. Beyond lies the pleasing hubbub of the Piazza del Duomo, with its cafés and restaurants, where young Prato shows off its designer tee-shirts and sweaters, and *motorini* buzz the unsuspecting stroller. The *pratesi* are of a different cast to the strapping Florentines, stockier and more Germanic. By no special coincidence, the town's gastronomic speciality is a tough yellow biscuit, cut in diagonal wedges and baked to a tooth-cracking hardness. *Biscotti di Prato* are an indispensable complement to an Italian Christmas and New Year, delicious when steeped in sweet wine (*vinsanto*) or coffee.

Leaving the town by the Florence road, turn northwards at Calenzano towards the range of mountain spurs along the edge of the River Sieve known as the Mugello. Part of a series of ancient lakes filling the Tuscany of ten million years ago, the region has an appealing ruggedness in its deeply-incised valleys and thickly-clustered woods, and has never quite lost its character as a primeval frontier. The Florentine grip on the whole territory, including the mountainous Pratomagno and Casentino further to the south, was assured through a series of fortified villages – *borghi* – stretching from Scarperia down to Terranuova Bracciolini, designed, or at any rate projected, by the indefatigable Arnolfo di Cambio, whose work provided the foundation for so much that we value in Florence itself.

The area was a nursery of artists: Fra Angelico was born at Vicchio, Paolo Uccello at Pratovecchio, Giotto came from the hamlet of Vespignano and Michelangelo's roots lay at Caprese in the mountains north of Arezzo. None of the places in this part of Tuscany, by its very nature, has been encumbered with masterpieces of painting or sculpture, but the element of good old-fashioned picturesque in the landscape, the dramatic setting of castles and convents 'in a gash of the wind-grieved Apennine' and a sort of homespun

stateliness in the layout and positioning of towns like Poppi and Bibbiena makes this one of the most arresting tracts of the whole province. It should not be missed by any traveller liking the challenge of mountain roads and the incentive offered by whatever lies around the next bend.

The Mugello was the ancestral territory of the Medici and it was Cosimo il Vecchio, known as Pater Patriae, who consolidated his family's hold on their northern estates after his final seizure of power in Florence in 1434. To do him justice, this was not simply because he appreciated the need for places of refuge and safety in the seesaw world of fifteenth-century politics, but also since, like so many tyrants before and afterwards, he was a simple, unpretending family man, who liked nothing better than a country life, alternating philosophical discussion with labour in his vineyards and harvest fields. Though his favourite villa was at Careggi, now in the very suburbs of Florence, he was almost as fond of Cafaggiolo and Trebbio, where the Medici children could be brought up in rustic security, away from the menace and sophistication of cities.

Reached after a drive along the edge of the Monti di Calvana, *il palazzo di Cafaggiolo in Mugello* is nowadays somewhat forlorn, falling apparently into general disrepair and only visible from the road. Michelozzo was the architect who, in 1451, transformed the existing fortress into something a trifle softer, with gardens and fountains 'and other things answerable to the honour of villas', as Vasari says, but the highjinks of the young Giulianos, Nanninas and Laudomias of its best days have gone and the place is a dingy old yellow carcass behind its fence.

To the south, a turning just above Novoli leads to Trebbio, which Michelozzo rebuilt some ten years later, still retaining its castellated exterior. On its hilltop, climbed in a magnificent sweep of Tuscan cypress, this is in far better shape than poor Cafaggiolo,

At Cosimo de Medici's beloved Cafaggiolo you
can see the way in which the villa evolved from
a fortress.

and open to visitors by prior arrangement on the first Tuesday of each month. Michelozzo's work for the Medici was prodigious and his stamp on renaissance Tuscany in city and country was among the most authoritative, but it is at the convent of Bosco ai Frati, folded deeply, almost invisibly, into its wooded valley (the name means 'Friars' Wood'), that his eloquent plainness strikes home with its unforced charm. The turn off the road beyond San Piero a Sieve is easily missed, and the edges of the tarmac surface shelve abruptly, so that the motorist can all too easily end up in the ditch, but the journey is always worth the risk.

Bosco ai Frati is a small Franciscan community, based on one of the oldest monastic retreats in this part of Italy, originating with a hermitage of exiled Greek monks founded in the seventh century but abandoned by the year 1012. It was St Francis himself who re-established a religious rule here two hundred years later, and it is not difficult to understand the appeal of the place for a spirit which drew inspiration so ardently from the natural world. Classic Franciscan ground, the convent nourished the redoubtable St Bonaventure, general of the Order, his piety making an indelible mark upon the young Dante, who exalts him in the *Paradiso*. Greeted by the Papal legates with the news that Pope Gregory X had made him a cardinal, Bonaventure was washing up the convent pots in the garden after a midday meal and only donned the hat and robes of his new eminence when the task was finished: the cherry tree where they hung is still shown.

The sober reconstruction of the convent undertaken by Michelozzo at Cosimo's behest – the Medici loved Bosco ai Frati and lavished gifts on it – was wholly in keeping with the simplicity essential to the Franciscan way. Here we never have that sense, sometimes strong in other Italian monasteries, that as soon as our backs are turned the reverend brothers will get out the card-pack and the *grappa* bottle. The vaulted rectory, the cloister and the washroom with its stone basins are components of a genuine *vita contemplativa*, whose spirit is perfectly conveyed by the wooden crucifix, once on the high altar of the chapel but now in the sacristy, almost certainly the work of Donatello (1382–1466).

Art historians are divided on the issue, but if Donatello did not make the cross, then he certainly should have done. Broken during an earthquake in 1542, it was cunningly repaired and stands as one of the most ferocious evocations of physical suffering in renaissance art. The heroic football captains and gymnastic champions of a thousand painted cruci-fixions are a world away, and the emaciated figure of Christ, lips parted in an agonized gasp, the lean, totally nude body bearing the weals of its scourging at the hands of the Roman legionaries, hangs in divine reproach from the cross, a Christ for hermits and visionaries looking beyond the earthly dimension.

Rejoining the main road at San Piero a Sieve, you move eastwards along the broad, flat river valley, keeping to the left bank of the Sieve itself as you pass through Borgo San Lorenzo and Rabatta to reach Vicchio on the flat top of its little hill. This was the birthplace in 1387 of one of Italy's best-loved painters, Fra Angelico, or, as he is often styled, with felicitous appropriateness, Il Beato Angelico. Blessed indeed he was, with an unrivalled gift for communicating the true beauty of holiness, without needing to be either mawkish or portentous about it. Most of his major works are in Florence, where he spent his life as a Dominican friar, his piety as celebrated as his art. Vicchio, alas, has none of his paintings and must content itself with a memorial inscription affixed to the Municipio in the Piazza Giotto. On Sunday afternoons there is a jolly little market in the tree-shaded Piazza della Vittoria, with stalls selling excellent dried and candied fruits.

The bushy, spiky Mugello countryside can be

Family coats of arms in terracotta decorate a wall at Borgo San Lorenzo.

become his apprentice. The result is for us to marvel at in Padua or Assisi.

Giotto's birthplace, an agreeably solid medieval farmhouse of mingled brick and stone, forms part of an enchanting group, a piece of the old travellers' Italy of engravings and watercolours. Shaded by a grove of beech and balsam poplar, the house is flanked by a plain country church smartened up in the days of the last Grand Duke, and a handsome white villa behind green gates; the charm of the ensemble is not at all Tuscan, but none the worse for that.

At Dicomano take the road up to the church of Santa Maria, as good an example as any of a country *parrocchiale* in this part of Tuscany. The custodian lets you in through the little cloister, cluttered with odd bits of ecclesiastical lumber, under the shadow of a pompous-looking bell-tower. Here, inside a simple romanesque box, is the agreeable and predictable *mélange* of terracottas from the school of della Robbia, rapidly disappearing baroque crusts and a couple of decent-to-average works from the variable hand of Santi di Tito (1538–1603), the prolific painter from Sansepolcro whose canvases are scattered up and down the locality.

At this point faint hearts may choose to turn back towards Florence, but the bold traveller will press on, taking the side road via Londa and Stia down the headwaters of the Arno. Fourth in depth and seventh in length among the rivers of Italy, this classic stream rises on the looming Monte Falterona, marking the frontier with Emilia Romagna. Its westward curve round Pratomagno, after a long easterly descent towards Arezzo, is as insolently unexpected as the notorious arc of the Niger which so confused early explorers. Italian rivers have little or nothing of the beauty of their northern sisters. What English heart has not sunk at the prospect of those dismal poplar-lined banks and stony shores littered with an archaeology of trash? The Arno, however, more than passes muster, as

glimpsed in Angelico's backgrounds, as in those of a yet more distinguished predecessor, greatest of all medieval painters, commemorated by a statue in Vicchio but born a little beyond the town in the hamlet of Vespignano, reached up a lane to the right of the main Dicomano road. Giotto di Bondone (*c.* 1266–1337) was a poor farmer's son, who amused himself with drawing while looking after his father's flock. Tradition says that the painter Cimabue, happening to pass through the village, found the boy sketching a sheep with one stone on another and invited him to

179

eighteenth-century travellers realized when they gave its name to elegant suburbs of London and Bristol called Arnos Grove and Arnos Vale, taking their cue from a phrase in Lord Middlesex's mourning ode on the last of the Medici.

The vales and hills of the upper Arno, the area known as the Casentino, are scattered with orchards and sheep pastures and the landscape perceptibly softens as the road bears southwards to Poppi. Historically this territory was divided between the bishops of Arezzo and the powerful Guidi family, whose castle at Romena is reached along the right-hand fork of the road out of Stia. Begun in the eleventh century, the fortress, now a well-kept ruin, was later the haunt of a skilful forger, Adamo da Brescia, whose counterfeit florins brought down terrible Florentine vengeance. No wealth could have compensated him for being burnt alive. Dante, here as a guest of the Guidi during his interminable exile's wanderings, commemorated the episode in Canto XXX of the *Inferno*. In 1902, in the little villa next to the castle, that monster of super-kitsch Gabriele d'Annunzio wrote part of his *Alcione* and carried on an affair with the actress Eleonora Duse, the pair of them doubtless inspired by Romena's towers and ramparts to dream up their stage farrago of fake medievalism, *Francesca da Rimini*.

At the foot of the hill is the exceedingly handsome *pieve*, said to be the oldest of its kind in the Casentino, dating from the mid twelfth century. With its thickset campanile and expansive arcading across the outer walls of the apse, its roomy nave and aisles, it is really more like a small cathedral than a country parish church. The atmosphere is as perfectly romanesque as you could wish, from the naked crossbeams of the roof to the inverted cup of the apsidal shell. It is reflected most powerfully in the primitive workmanship of the capitals, journeyman sculpture with the customary motifs of angels, staring faces and animal shapes picked out in jagged, gawky relief. The first pillar to the right of the entrance carries an inscription announcing that 'Albericus the parish priest made this work', while the second to the left says that it took place 'in a time of famine 1152'. Best among the pictures is an anonymous fifteenth-century *Madonna with Saints* in the north aisle.

As you follow the road to Poppi, running parallel with the single-track railway from Stia to Arezzo, you pass the fateful battlefield of Campaldino on the right. Here, on 11 June 1289, the Tuscan Ghibellines, marching out from Arezzo in support of the Emperor, were decisively defeated by the Guelph forces from Florence, an army which included the 24-year-old Dante. He never forgot the experience of the battle, raging doubtfully on throughout the day, and worked memories of it into the *Divina Commedia*.

A sight of Poppi on its hilltop is unforgettable, and so is the serpentine drive across the river and up the steep slopes into the town, past an odd-looking Fascist belvedere-cum-war-memorial and under the city

Left Dante's familiar hawk-nosed profile contemplates the Casentino, where he sought refuge during his exile.

Above A deceptively simple exterior conceals some florid baroque decoration in the Madonna del Morbo, Poppi.

walls, pierced here and there with the elegant windows of the houses they have subsumed. The place has all the impacted grandeur of a Tuscan *borgo*, its churches, palaces and fortifications squeezed together like a half-kneaded cake. It is best to park outside the walls and walk up to the Piazza Amerighi, which contains in its midst what looks like the butter-cross of an English market town but is in fact the skittishly baroque Madonna del Morbo, its dome and porticoes and white and gilt stucco interior commemorating Poppi's delivery from plague in 1631.

This forms a natural close to the vista along the arcaded Via Cavour, whose arches, having been put up at different stages, offer a perverse visual amusement. At the bottom, like an old dog which has given up fighting to lie in the sun, is the battered fourteenth-century church of San Fedele, with a handful of paintings whose quality is concealed by a film of decay. Here too lies the town's patron saint, the Franciscan evangelist Torello who died in 1282.

What gives Poppi its true character, however, is the bristling Palazzo Pretorio on a plateau at the top of the hill. This was the stronghold of the Guidi, strong enough indeed to hold out until 1440 against Florentine domination. Across the moat the almost blank crenellated walls with their tremendous watch-tower in the western corner shelter a narrow quadrangle stuck haphazardly with *stemme* (coats of arms) of the various lords, from Simone di Battifolle, who built the castle in 1274, to Florentine governors of the sixteenth century. Restoration of the interior, which includes an ancient library and a chapel frescoed by Taddeo Gaddi (1300–66), has been indefinitely postponed and the exquisite galleried

---

The olive characterizes the Tuscan landscape from north to south, though recent hard winters have destroyed many trees.

staircase is tantalizingly fenced off from visitors.

The logical chaser to Poppi is Bibbiena, a handshaking distance across the luridly green valley, but there is no reason not to strike off into the deep Apennines in search of Camaldoli, one of the most famous of all the hermitages with which this corner of Tuscany is crammed. Perhaps take time to savour the chestnut-flour pancakes stuffed with ricotta at the restaurant in Moggiona on the way.

Fleshly pleasures were to be eschewed when Count Maldolo of Arezzo gave the whole of this superb tract of ancient forest to San Romualdo – or St Rumbold as he used to be called in England – the patron saint of stammerers, in 1012 for the creation of a hermitage. Maldolo's name stuck to the place and so did the devotion of the hermits themselves, systematized into a sub-order of the Benedictines some thirty years after Romualdo's death.

Their cells, like cosy bungalows on a housing estate, form a little enclave to the north of the monastery church. Nearly all of them date from the sixteenth century, results of aristocratic piety and penitence: the Cella della Madonna di Loreto, for instance, lodged St Charles Borromeo, the Cella di San Paolo sheltered the Venetian patrician Tommaso Giustiniani, and the Cella di Medici was built by a Medici princess at the bidding of her relative Pope Leo X as an act of repentance for having tried to get into the hermitage in male disguise.

Women are indeed not allowed to set foot in these cells or in the adjacent monastery, though they may enter the chapel, whose chaste baroque façade shows St Romualdo and Benedict flanking the Saviour (the building is of 1708). The life of these white-robed cenobites ordains an abstention from meat, seven hours' sleep and chanting the psalms at half past one each morning. Further down the mountain, in the monastery itself, one of those old fortress convents like the great Saint Bernard in Switzerland, the exterior's prison-like grimness conceals one of the most exquisite

all not open + restored (1995)

183

of Italian cloister gardens, bright with geraniums, hollyhocks and roses, and protected, unusually, by glazed screens across its arches. The monastic pharmacy, besides producing the usual revoltingly sweet liqueur, has the magic of ancient quackery about it, full of big-bellied carboys and alembics, stuffed birds, wondrous shells, crucibles and pots for chemical stinks, flower presses and antique herbals with crackling pages. The brothers are still out there under the huge beech trees and stands of oak and chestnut, gathering simples like any old Friar Lawrence, when not worshipping amid the abstracted dignity of Vasari's canvases on the walls of the church.

A dull road takes you down through workaday Soci to climb up again to Bibbiena, a place of far greater size and consequence than might at first appear. It was important enough in the twelfth century to be mentioned by the Arab geographer Idrisi, and may have been in existence as Vibenna in Etruscan times. Anyone fond of the theatre, and more particularly of sumptuous baroque and rococo stage design, will know it as the home ground of the great family of the Bibiena (for some reason they only have one 'b'), which produced the most inspired scene painters of seventeenth- and eighteenth-century Europe. Theatrical associations cling as strongly to the palace in Via Dovizi, topped by a loggia over a row of oddly Moorish-looking windows, which belonged to Benedetto Dovizi, 'cardinal Bibbiena'. Secretary to Pope Leo X and patron of Raphael, he was also the author of *La Calandria*, a pioneering vernacular comedy which, however indirectly, influenced those of Shakespeare.

Opposite the palace is the impenetrably dark church of San Lorenzo, with some good terracotta panels of the

---

The town of Bibbiena, at the southern end of the Casentino, is one of the oldest in this part of Tuscany.

della Robbia school, a *Deposition* and a lively *Adoration of the Shepherds*. More interesting is SS Ippolito e Donato, reached up the sloping main drag of the town, which debouches into the broad Piazza Tarlati. Here are the remains of the old citadel converted into a clock-tower, and an ample prospect, from the northern end, of the country towards Poppi. The church itself possesses an unusual shape, more mosque than basilica, owing to various rebuildings, and contains three arresting pictures, an opulent altarpiece of 1435 by Bicci di Lorenzo, a Giottesque *Madonna and Child* by a fourteenth-century master, and an absorbing treatment of the same subject by Arcangelo di Cola (*c.* 1420), whose markedly different handling of colour and line belongs across the mountains in the luminous traditions of medieval painting in the Marche region.

From Bibbiena take the road back to Poppi and at Borgo alla Collina turn off left into the hills. From Montemignaio the road lurches down through thick deciduous forests to the monastery of Vallombrosa, founded here in 1038 by Giovanni Gualberto Visdomini as part of a sustained act of penitence which he had begun by pardoning his brother's murderer. Giovanni established a Benedictine sub-order which at its height held fifty monasteries, and after a long period of suppression it was reinstated here in 1963. The decoration of the monastery, mostly fair-to-middling baroque, is less remarkable than the woods which crowd in upon it. These certainly impressed the poet Milton, whose extensive Italian tour included a visit here in 1638. Years later, when describing the gathering devils in *Paradise Lost*, he portrayed them crowding

Thick as autumnal leaves that strow the brooks
In Vallombrosa, where th'Etrurian shades,
High-overarch'd, imbower.

I wonder why it is that all Milton's Tuscan memories seem to end up by being associated with Satan?

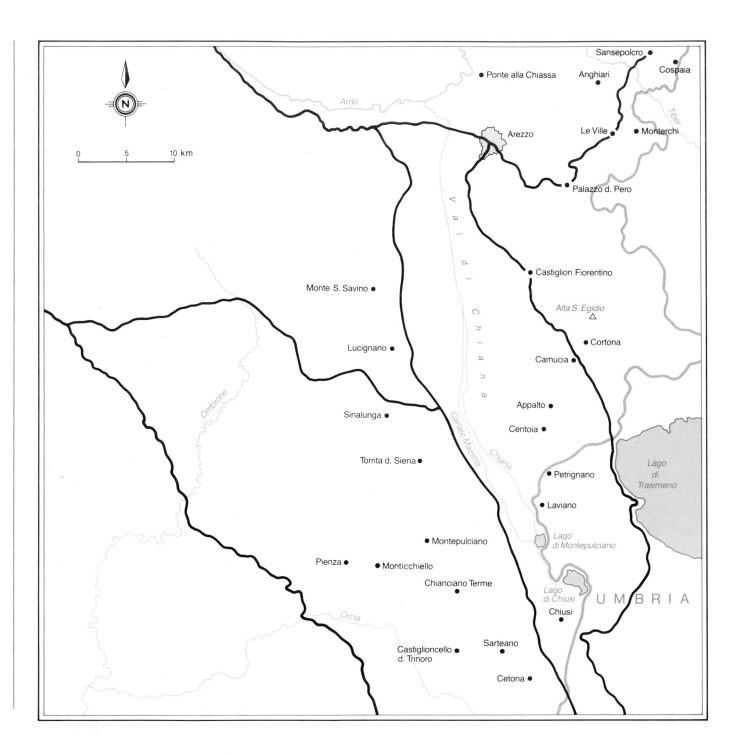

6
Arezzo and the South-East

Arezzo – Sansepolcro – Castiglion Fiorentino –
Cortona – Lago di Trasimeno – Chiusi –
Val d'Orcia – Montepulciano – Sinalunga –
Monte San Savino

Flung up against its steep hillside, Arezzo seems like one of those people whose bed or armchair may be excruciatingly uncomfortable, but who would never do anything so vulgar as to complain. The streets teeter and lurch, most of the more consequential buildings are approached by carefully angled steps and the principal square is a kind of elegant escarpment, yet the city, one of Tuscany's oldest inhabited sites, triumphantly vindicates its position, taking a justifiable pride in its gifts to the region and the world.

I love this place for its quality of uncompromising, self-confident individuality. There is something grandly distinctive in all its monuments, a background to new ideas and exciting initiatives, and this elemental originality emerges powerfully in its great men. These range from Maecenas, the noble patron of Horace and Virgil, Petrarch the poet and scholar linking the Middle Ages to the Renaissance, and Vasari, unrivalled memorialist of Italian painting, to figures such as the witty, bawdy letter-writer and dramatist Pietro Aretino and the wonderfully various baroque virtuoso Francesco Redi. Its history, from foundation as one of the principal strongholds of Etruria to its desperate year of resistance against the invading French in the 'Viva Maria' revolt of

1799–1800, is one of sturdy defiance, and it only yielded to the Florentines in 1384 as the result of a sordid deal for 40,000 florins with the French soldier of fortune Enguerrand de Coucy.

Any visit to Arezzo must begin with Piero della Francesca's stupendous fresco cycle *The Invention of the True Cross* in the church of San Francesco. Volumes have been written about these frescoes, but nobody has ever satisfactorily explained their grip on the beholder, and they are, in a sense, beyond the reach of analysis. Filling the presbytery of the huge preaching-barn of San Francesco, they were begun as a continuation of a project originally assigned to Bicci di Lorenzo, whose death in 1452 left only the outer arch, with its visions of Paradise, Purgatory and Hell, and a few figures completed.

Over the next fourteen years Piero (1406–92), inspired by the famous *Golden Legend* of Jacopo de Voragine, an anthology of lives of the saints, worked at a series of scenes embodying the ideal fulfilment of God's promises to mankind in the Old Testament through the events of the New, relating these to historical episodes surrounding the triumph of Christianity in the reign of the Emperor Constantine. The death of Adam and the visit of the Queen of Sheba

to Solomon (she is said to have prophesied that a bridge-timber later utilized in building the Temple would become the True Cross) are thus linked with the Dream of Constantine, the Battle of the Milvian Bridge through which he came to power, and the Annunciation to the Blessed Virgin, a link made all the stronger by the wealth of learned allusion intrinsic to Piero's handling of his theme.

Setting this aside, what holds us most powerfully, apart from the drama of light through darkness as the emperor lies asleep in his pavilion amid the watching sentries, or the brilliance of the cloud-flecked skies as the sweating workmen toil to raise the beam, is the strength in the hands and feet of Piero's figures and a sense in each face that its owner has been given some kind of intuition whose springs still elude us. These brawny labourers half stripped of their rumpled clothes, the Virgin, a dignified giantess under her marble portico, the unimaginably ancient Adam and Eve, all inhabit a world which has attained to a more intense reality than that of the thousands who look up at its bomb-damaged surfaces through the gloom of the half-ruined basilica.

From San Francesco turn left along the Via Cavour, which opens out into the Piazza della Badia. The Badia itself is the old abbey church of SS Flora and Lucilla, with a baroque campanile clapped on to one end and a charming cloister, whose refectory contains an enormous *Feast of Esther and Ahasuerus* by Vasari. He also painted the lofty, proportion-scorning canvas above the high altar, showing Christ calling Peter and Andrew from a faintly classicized punt on a Galilee surrounded by Roman ruins.

The Via Cavour's upward curve leads to the Via S. Lorentino, where the city's art gallery in the Palazzo Bruni holds a good assemblage of fifteenth- and sixteenth-century majolica and some decent late renaissance pictures, though the vagaries of *opera in restauro* mean that it is often shut. Among the painters represented is Giorgio Vasari and it is really him we are in search of, staggering up the Via XX Settembre towards the house he bought in 1540 and decorated as befitted one of the most learned and versatile, though scarcely the most inspired, of his artistic generation.

Born in Arezzo in 1511, he was taught drawing by his grandfather's cousin Luca Signorelli before being taken to Florence by a passing cardinal and ending up as the doyen of the Florentine art world in the confident decades of Grand Duke Cosimo I, who died in the same year, 1574. He was a better architect than painter, and far greater than both in his opinionated, enthusiastic series of artistic biographies, with its fascinating introductory attempt to create a historical context for the development of Italian painting and sculpture. In 1540, having bought his house here in Arezzo, he set out to decorate it in high style, and by common consent the work is the best he ever did, an uninhibited frolic through the late renaissance territory of emblem and allegory, with Peace, Concord, Virtue and Modesty taking charge of the nuptial bedroom, Vasari's wife Niccolosa Bacci as the muse of conjugal love in the Chamber of Apollo and delightful little portrait tributes to friends and mentors, including Michelangelo and Andrea del Sarto in the Chamber of Fame.

At the northern end of the street, a few steps to the right, is Piazza Fossombroni, where the unadorned gothic of San Domenico hides a looming and dramatic Cimabue crucifix. The square takes its name from one of the greatest of enlightened Tuscans, yet another Aretine, Vittorio Fossombroni, whose work in draining and fertilizing the marshy Val di Chiana, on the duchy's southern corner, was completed after the Napoleonic wars. For this *bonifica*, his master Grand Duke Ferdinand III received the tribute of a fine neo-

---

Sun and shadow stripe an Arezzo street.

The arms of a Medici pope strike a note of authority in Arezzo.

For a start, there is the rare joy in Italy of good painted glass, by the French monk Guillaume de Marcillat, whose work here during the 1520s included the frescoes in the nave vaulting, finished off a century later by Salvi Carlucci. There is the weirdly impressive early nineteenth-century chapel of the Madonna del Conforto, clamouring for attention behind its wrought-iron screen, with two excellent Andrea della Robbia terracottas rubbing shoulders with the romantic effusions of painters such as Pietro Benvenuti and Giuseppe del Rosso, living and working in Arezzo during the stirring, bloodthirsty days of the 'Viva Maria' revolt (see p. 187). There is the crocketed late medieval fantasy of the Arca di San Donato, the saint's reliquary, in the chancel, and Giotto's monument to the great Archbishop Tarlati in the north aisle to complement it. Finally, at the west end of the same aisle, high up on the wall, is the bewigged bust of Francesco Redi, the archetypal all-rounder and a true son of Tuscany.

That liveliest of travellers Lady Morgan (her Christian name was Sidney and she wrote an autobiographical novel called *The Wild Irish Girl*) noted that Arezzo's 'subtle air has been particularly favourable to genius; and in fact, under many moral disadvantages, it has produced men of eminent talent'. With few moral disadvantages and much talent, Redi, born here in 1626, went to Florence to become Cosimo III's doctor, and soon got to know everything and everyone worth knowing. He was a philologist, speaking and studying languages from Catalan to Arabic, a collector of manuscripts and curios, and a reliable go-between in dismal, bigoted Cosimo's scraps with his fractious family. He challenged the prevailing

classical statue by Stefano Ricci (1763–1837) at the top of nearby Via Sassoverde. Elsewhere in Italy this might have been swept away after Unification, but Tuscans have good cause to remember their former sovereigns with affectionate respect.

A left turn from the marble Ferdinand leads straight up to the broad irregular square in front of the *duomo*. For various reasons this is one of my favourite Tuscan cathedrals: a touch or two of gothic leavens the eternal romanesque, on whose charms I am sometimes heretical. The axiom that simple equals beautiful need not always hold true, and as one gloomy, homespun *pieve* succeeds another, I pine for a little more sophistication and variety, which the present building unfailingly offers.

The thirteenth-century apse of Santa Maria Assunta, seen from Palazzo dei Tribunali in Piazza Grande, Arezzo.

belief in the spontaneous generation of insects, wrote a study of vipers and examined human lice under his microscope. For an intensely religious man he was notably free from prejudice, and all good Tuscans know him as the author of that incomparable hymn to wine and food, *Bacco in Toscana*.

If lunchtime arrives as you leave the cathedral, the large semicircular Passeggio del Prato behind it offers a pleasant spot for a picnic, where a glass of the dry Chianti dei Colli Aretini or the rather acid Bianco Vergine di Valdichiana can be drunk to Redi's memory as you gaze out across the steep valley falling away below. Those in search of restaurant fare may treat themselves to *pappardelle alla lepre*, the pasta with hare sauce which, though nowadays universal in Tuscany, belongs officially to Arezzo, *frittata affogata*, a sort of vegetable omelette with basil and parsley, or the stew of mixed game, veal, pork and chicken known as *scottiglia*.

Downhill walking is now in order, and flights of steps lead comfortably into Piazza Grande. The gradient principle of Arezzo's layout is perfectly illustrated here, in a square whose effect depends on a sequence of angles and slopes. The buildings around it encompass an entire history of Italian architecture from romanesque to renaissance. On the northern edge stands Vasari's nobly porticoed Palazzo delle Logge, with shops underneath its tall arches, and at right-angles to this lies the amazingly effective synthesis of the Palazzo della Fraternità dei Laici. The lower half of the palace is delicate gothic of 1377 by Baldino di Cino and Niccolò di Francesco, with an upper storey completed in 1435 by Bernardo Rossellino (1409–64), rounded off a century later by a felicitous little triple-arched campanile by Felice di Salvatore da Fossato. Next door is the Palazzo dei Tribunali, straight from Berninian Rome, and beyond it the broad romanesque apsidal curve of the old Pieve di Santa Maria faces an engaging scatter of medieval houses.

Despite my unkind remarks about the effects of too much romanesque, I must go cap in hand before the *pieve*, with its campanile forming an accent over the city's skyline. It has the only truly arresting church façade in Arezzo, as good as anything at Lucca, Pisa or Pistoia, with vigorous sculptured reliefs of the months. These are especially powerful towards the year's end, where one man gathers turnips and another slaughters a pig. Inside there is an abrupt theatricality in the light from the windows and the height of the galleried presbytery above a deeply incised crypt. The darkness holds a silver reliquary bust of San Donato, workmanship of singular beauty by two Aretine craftsmen named Pietro and Paolo, who made it in 1346.

The saint was bishop here during the early fifth century and owed his martyrdom (by decapitation) to a panic wave of pagan apostasy, a reaction to the gothic invasion of Italy. On the high altar overhead he figures beside the Baptist, St Matthew and St John the Evangelist in a quartet of saints adoring the Madonna and Child in Pietro Lorenzetti's polyptych of 1312, a perfect synthesis of all the tenderness, radiance and fluidity essential to the greatest Sienese art.

Nearly all the approach roads to Arezzo are insufferably straight and dull, but if you are still reeling from the splendours of Piero and in search of more, it is worth risking the Bibbiena road as far as Ponte alla Chiassa before turning eastwards to Anghiari. This is sunflower and tobacco country, the former having become very popular owing to EEC subsidies and stippling the valleys of eastern Tuscany with cheerful flecks of garish yellow. The latter was grown extensively during the nineteenth century in the neighbouring Papal States – indeed the little village of Cospaia just over the border was almost an autonomous republic in its successful contraband balancing act between Pope and Grand Duke – but now its long light-green clumps are everywhere.

This agricultural patchwork can be seen across the fat alluvial plain of the young Tiber from the centre of Anghiari, whose spectacular lookout post commands a dramatic vista as far as Sansepolcro on the further river bank. Admirers of Leonardo will know his cartoon and studies for an unachieved painting of the battle which took place here in 1440 between the Florentines and the army of Filippo Maria Visconti, Duke of Milan, resulting in Florence's annexation of the town. Though there is little in the way of individual works of art in this hilltop eyrie, Anghiari itself is so attractive, with its narrow, tumbling streets, haphazard flights of steps and sudden glimpses of the country through the curve of an arch or down the plunge of a lane bright with potted geraniums, that it is worth a stroll, and lunch, maybe, off the local variety of spaghetti, *bringoli*, in sausage sauce.

One of the very best Tuscan lunches, however, is to be had at Sansepolcro, in the cool darkness of the Le Albergo Fiorentino. As a dire onslaught of *nouvelle cuisine*, fast food, dieting fads and fitness crazes lays siege to the sacred gastronomic rites of Italy, it is a blessed relief to find places like this still in the business of providing the true savours and textures of Italian food without fuss or pretence. What is more, in view of the grotesque prices charged in many more illustrious but infinitely less satisfying Tuscan haunts, it is all admirably inexpensive.

And there is far more to this ancient place than lunch. Sansepolcro, or Borgo Sansepolcro as it is still often called, was the birthplace of Piero della Francesca, whose house, where he wrote his treatise on perspective, can still be seen in the Via Matteotti. A few steps along the street is the Palazzo Comunale, which contains two of his very finest works, the awe-inspiring *Resurrection* of 1463 and the inscrutably vatic *Madonna della Misericordia* of some fifteen years earlier. Both pictures are of the kind which look at us as we look at them. This risen Christ and presiding Madonna are icons of no particularized faith but of the essential religious impulses of mankind, here before names were given to deities and destined to outlast all the sects, bigotries and contentions by which Christianity has ever been fragmented. Their creator understood the fear as well as the mystery within true devotion, and the setting of a provincial art gallery does nothing to diminish that.

Sheila Hale, writer of the best short guide to Tuscany, calls Sansepolcro 'this somewhat mournful town'. I disagree: quiet, a trifle solemn it may always seem, this Medici purchase from the Pope, but the soft yellow and pinkish grey of its palaces and churches is anything but sad, as though Piero's reflective calm had somehow or other got out of the museum and diffused itself through the fabric of the place.

One more work of his must be seen on this pilgrimage, the unforgettable *Madonna del Parto* at Monterchi. Taking the main Arezzo road, turn off at Le Ville to the foot of the hill on which Monterchi itself stands. In the valley below, a track leads up to a cemetery, one of those high-walled Italian graveyards where families lie stacked in what look like marble chests-of-drawers studded with oval photographs of many a plump-cheeked mamma and jowly papa and their handsome offspring. A small chapel to one side contains Piero's stunning image of triumphant pregnancy (*parto* means childbirth), with the blue-gowned Virgin appreciatively fingering her belly as attendant angels look on.

At Palazzo di Pero, a dozen kilometres further on, veer south towards Castiglion Fiorentino, impressively sited above the flat green spread of the Val di Chiana. This is the valley of the sluggish River Chiana, formerly a pestiferous swamp but later enriched by two centuries of Medicean *bonifica* and the construction of a substantial canal, the Fosso Maestro, to create what is nowadays one of the most abundantly fertile regions of Tuscany. A grand prospect of the

193

plain and the dominant cone of Monte Amiata beyond is gained from the old tower at the centre of Castiglion Fiorentino itself, whose fortunes tossed to and fro from Arezzo to Perugia and the Papacy until Florence assumed control in 1384. Apart from the windswept charm of the town, with its Vasarian loggia in the Piazza del Municipio, the churches hold good things, including a Lorenzo di Credi (1459–1537), at his most winsome, of a *Virgin and Saint Joseph adoring the Christ Child*, in the Collegiata (do not be put off by the neo-classical restoration) and a frescoed *Deposition* by Luca Signorelli on the left-hand wall of what remains of the ancient *pieve*. As for the art gallery opposite the loggia, it is one of those Tuscan small-town 'omnium gatherum' affairs which I so enjoy for their higgledy-piggledy unexpectedness – crusts a-plenty, but a handful of objects as always to redeem disappointment and make us realize the sheer prodigality of talent and taste in this part of Italy.

So down beside the railway line to Cortona, last city of any consequence before the frontier of the Papal States. The place has an importance out of all proportion to its extent. Nobody seems to know who really began it, but a town was already in existence by the time the Etruscans arrived in the region during the sixth century BC, and Roman writers subsequently attributed its foundation to Corythus, father of Dardanus, ancestor of the Trojans, thus making it hoary in the extreme. From its days as part of one of the Etruscan *lucumones*, a confederation of twelve cities, there survive fragments of 'cyclopean' walling of a kind seen to better advantage at Volterra, but easily glimpsed here in the western stretch of ramparts by the Porta Santa Maria. On the road up from the railway at Camucia a scatter of tombs known to local inhabitants

---

An Impressionist painting produced by nature in a Tuscan field.

as '*meloni*' from their domed tops shows that we are well and truly within the Etruscan territory which ultimately gave a name to Tuscany.

Cortona's position, on the edge of the mountain spur of Alta Sant' Egidio, is spectacular enough. Where Arezzo has a sublime awkwardness and Siena has snuggled down into its high crater, Cortona looks shamelessly lofty and dominant. Spending a night here, with the lights of the villages in twinkling patches across the blackness below, is like being on the deck of a ship which will sooner or later set off in stately progress through the dark, so that you never quite know where you might wake up next morning.

Not all travellers have loved the place as it deserves. Maurice Hewlett, a best-selling Edwardian novelist unread nowadays, burst out in splenetic rage at it in 1904 – 'undeniably Tuscan, mountain-built, harsh and uncomfortable as nearly all hill-towns in Tuscany are'. The road was too tortuous and the single inn was perfectly foul. 'The host and his wife are obsequious but helpless; the entrance swarms with beggars and touts', though the chambermaid was 'a young and pretty woman, with the most exuberant person I ever saw in this world'. Poor Hewlett! The guide he hired was a liar who showed him derelict churches with pictures 'cracking, dropping and clouded with cobwebs'. No wonder he wrote the whole thing off as 'drab and dingy, stinking city . . . I never was in a viler-smelling town'. It need hardly be said that this has all changed, if it ever was so anyway. The Oasi and San Michele are excellent hotels, you can eat well at the Loggetta in Piazza Pescheria or at the more crowded Tonino in Piazza Garibaldi, and as for smells they are far more likely to be that olfactory cocktail of Italian streets, made up of roasting coffee, newly-baked bread, fresh paint and exhaust fumes, with – well, perhaps – the occasional whiff of a drain to add character to the experience.

What the traveller to Cortona will need, however, is

a strong pair of legs. The hills are some of the steepest in a Tuscan city and many of the buildings are approached by dramatic flights of steps, though these give an additional sweep to a place already rich in visual rewards. The Palazzo Comunale in Piazza della Repubblica is a typical example: enlarged in the sixteenth century from the original structure of 1275, it cries out for some Verdian or Donizettian *melodramma* to take place on the platform at the top of its broad stone stairway. The piazza itself is part of an exciting sequence of open spaces stretching north-west as far as the cathedral and ramparts. Due north is Piazza Signorelli, where the Palazzo Casali has one of the region's best Etruscan collections, whose treasures, including an Attic vase showing Hercules strangling the Nemean lion and an immense bronze lamp decorated with cheerfully lustful flute-blowing Silenuses (attendants on Bacchus) and contrastingly demure Sirens, display the more cosmopolitan tastes of the Val di Chiana's ancient masters.

This museum belongs to the Accademia Etrusca, founded in 1727 by three brothers of the Venuti family. They also initiated a splendid library, among whose 45,000 volumes is the manuscript of the *Laudario di Cortona*, a series of hauntingly beautiful hymns of praise and penitence in honour of the Blessed Virgin. Composed during the last decades of the thirteenth century, the *laudi* celebrated the Madonna in the fervent idiom of secular love poetry:

> *Diana, stella lucente,*
> *letizia de tutta la gente,*
> *tutto lo mondo è perdente*
> *senza la tua vigoria.*
> *Vigorosa, potente, beata,*
> *per te è questa laude cantata.*

> Diana, blazing star,
> happiness of the whole world,
> everything is lost
> without your strength.
> Vigorous, powerful, blessed,
> this song of praise is for you.

– the ideal counterpart to the graces of Duccio and Simone Martini.

Public spirit has played a strong part in Cortona's life. Opposite the palace are a handsome nineteenth-century theatre and cornmarket loggia from the last grand-ducal days of Leopold II, and from here it is an easy step through the Piazza Trento e Trieste to the curving square in front of the renaissance *duomo*, attributed to Giuliano da Sangallo but more likely to be by a pupil. Visit the rewarding Museo Diocesano here, knocked together from two churches joined by a substantial stairway. In the upper church the best things are surely the wonderful Fra Angelico *Annunciation*, in which the beauty of the angel's wings makes them almost audible, a *Madonna and Child with Angels and Saints* by Sassetta, the memorably idiosyncratic Sienese who, despite Sir John Pope Hennessy's great study, published almost half a century ago, is not nearly well known enough to lovers of Italian art, an anguished *Crucifixion* by Pietro Lorenzetti (*d.* 1350) and a noble handful of works by Luca Signorelli, including a *Nativity* and a *Deposition*.

Signorelli was born at Cortona in 1441 and has always been famous as 'the precursor of Michelangelo'. A dreadful label, and one which he does not deserve. His richly personal style, with its unmistakable handling of colour and outline, best known from the frescoes in Orvieto cathedral, is something of an acquired taste. Trollope's heroines, reluctant to accept potential husbands, are urged by their mammas to 'learn to love him' and we ought to learn to love Luca.

The quality of mysterious, arcane paganism in his manner surely derived from this most rustic corner of Etruria, with the gods of Umbria's lakes and woodlands just over the mountain's brow.

Past the stately palace fronts of Via Dardano and Via Benedetti – the great families of Cortona built with taste as well as pomp – you arrive at San Francesco, a nice muddle of gothic and baroque. The ivory Byzantine reliquary on the high altar contains a sliver of the True Cross and a side chapel on the north side houses an *Annunciation*, the last, unfinished work of the city's second great painter, Pietro Berettini, known to us as Pietro da Cortona (1596–1669). Pious prejudice against the Italian baroque dies hard, but only fools and prigs still kick against the world of brilliant colour and flamboyant design created by this protean talent, whose finest flourishes are in his frescoes for the churches and palaces of Rome.

His birthplace is in Via Berettini, running up from San Francesco past San Niccolò, which contains a large processional banner decorated by Signorelli, to the basilica of Santa Margherita. Every Italian town boasts its local saint, and Margherita di Laviano is a most attractive tutelary presence. A medieval farmer's daughter, she had a harsh childhood and fell in love, aged 17, with a young knight who promised marriage. They lived together out of wedlock in Montepulciano a few miles south-west until one evening when he failed to return home and their faithful dog led her to his dead body. Distracted with grief, she wandered off to Cortona with her little son and spent the rest of her life ministering to the sick and the poor of the city. She lies now in a silver urn designed by Pietro da Cortona, but a grander memorial is the delicate gothic tomb made for her in 1362 by Angelo and Francesco di Pietro.

Unlike Maurice Hewlett, most of us leave Cortona reluctantly, and each of its six gates holds something to keep the traveller back. Outside the Porta Colonia, for example, is the pretty little box of Santa Maria Nuova, Vasari improving on Cristofanello and a dome clapped fancifully on top a century afterwards. In San Domenico, near the Porta Berarda, are frescoes by Signorelli and Fra Angelico, and on the hillside below the Porta Sant'Agostino stands the cleanly proportioned Madonna del Calcinaio of 1484–1513.

Searchers after the Etruscans can take the road south via Appalto and Centoia, cutting across an Umbrian corner at Petrignano, with Lake Trasimeno a grey-green blur below. Past Margherita's home village of Laviano (or Alviano), turn sharp left at the main junction, down to Chiusi.

Etruscan Camars, Roman Clusium, stronghold of Lars Porsenna, against whom Horatius kept the bridge, Chiusi has never recovered from the scars of medieval warfare and the resulting devastation and depopulation of the Val di Chiana. A small agricultural town on a plug of tufa above a little lake, it has one of the most romantic prospects in Tuscany, with Cortona clearly visible on her north-eastern perch, the wooded Umbrian hills to the south, and westward the stark ridges of Monte Amiata. As so often happens in these places of decayed splendour, the cathedral has retained traces of workmanship from the days of the Longobards, Italy's Germanic rulers Christianized in the sixth century, when Chiusi was a dukedom. Though dedicated to St Secondianus, the church also holds the body of another Roman martyr, St Mustiola, beaten to death with a cat-o'-nine-tails in AD 275 for spurning the provincial governor's lustful advances.

You can confront the Etruscans at second hand in the National Archaeological Museum next to the cathedral, which interestingly fuses local discoveries with Greek and Roman artefacts to make a suitable context. Amid the attic vases and senatorial busts are the weirdly sightless, hypothalamic gazes of Etruscan funerary effigies, seated women, recumbent men, their names so eloquently neither Latin nor Greek – 'Thania

Above Lake Trasimeno, where Tuscany ends and Umbria begins.

Right A farmhouse near Chiusi. The topmost storey was used as a dovecote.

Rusina', 'Larth Sentinates Caesa', 'Avle Vpna'. Many of the grave goods come from the tombs in the oak groves between the town and the lake, of which the most notable are the Tomba della Pellegrina and the Tomba della Scimmia. The former, dating from around 300 BC, consists of an oval chamber with a long corridor, containing urns in niches representing mythological scenes, while the latter, uncovered in 1846, has a whole sequence of magnificent paintings on its tufa walls, including an energetic chariot race and vigorous nude youths.

Avoiding the main road to Chianciano, turn south for a far more attractive route to Montepulciano along the edge of Val d'Orcia, a country of dense olive groves and broad stands of oak and broom, whose explosions puncture the rasping of the cicadas in the summer heat. Cetona lurched back and forth from Emperor and Pope to Florentine and Sienese, but its cypress and pine-girdled fortress has long since been softened into a garden belvedere from which there are views across to the long, straight ridge of the town's eponymous mountain.

Sarteano, on its travertine plateau, is not much more than a village with palaces, and the lovelier because of it. The place seems to be hinting at a grander destiny, but when you reach the great *rocca* at the top of the Corso Garibaldi you understand why this never came about. Over the main doorway is the suckling she-wolf of Siena, whose dominion in this part of Tuscany nearly always meant crippling taxes and wholesale neglect of the local economy. Thus Sarteano sleeps on, with its tunnel-like *vicoli*, its stretches of Etruscan wall from the days when it was 'Pagus Sartheanus' and, in the church of San Francesco, its one outstanding picture, an *Annunciation* by the genial Sienese eccentric Domenico Beccafumi.

Out of Sarteano, turn westwards along the exceedingly minor and thoroughly enjoyable road to Castiglioncello and Chiarentana. You are now above a valley made famous by one of the finest books ever to come out of the terrible scourge inflicted on Italy by the Germans after Mussolini's fall in 1943. Iris Origo's *War in Val d'Orcia* was based on the diaries she kept while chatelaine of La Foce. With grim courage she hid escaped prisoners in the garden, handed refugees along the next stage of their 'underground railroad', dealt coolly with trigger-happy German soldiers and fractious Italian partisans, listened to the rumble of gunfire and bombing in the neighbouring valleys, yet somehow contrived to relish the change of the Tuscan seasons and the immemorial rhythms of peasant farming.

Nowadays this entire south-eastern tract of the province is the smart end of Tuscany for arty Italians in the up-market reaches of the media, entertainment and design worlds. If every vineyard and cypress in the Chianti hides a Brit, down here during the summer come Milanese journalists, music critics and actors, fashion arbiters and the sort of bookish American, German or Australian eager to escape the swimming-pool Sloane Rangers of Radda and Greve.

Many of these people converge each year on Montepulciano, whose July festival is the result of a singular initiative during the 1970s by the composer Hans Werner Henze, designed to bring the people of the local community into direct contact with art through participation in recitals and dramatic spectacle. Now that Marx and Mao are no longer Italy's flavour-of-the-month, the occasion's more *engagé* aspects have largely disappeared, but it still offers an exciting programme, centred on the sort of operatic and concert rarities which form the typical fare of Italian summer festivals.

Tuscany rolls south towards the Umbrian frontier in a series of gentle wooded hills.

Excuses of this kind are scarcely necessary for visiting Montepulciano. How can anyone not love this place? Here, more perhaps than anywhere else in Tuscany, it is possible to feel the nap and grain on the surface of an Italian town and luxuriate in the blending of its colours, as if it were some cherished animal whose coat you delighted to stroke. The travertine, a calcareous tufa which looks like sponge cake, has none of that staring whiteness of northern marble, and the brick, far from an unvarying red, is russet, ochre, pink, madder or mauve. The city was not so much built as grown and moulded, its streets and buildings shaped into the kind of harmony whose perfection is at times almost intolerable. When the traveller reaches the point at which he finds himself wanting to *be* Montepulciano, then he knows it is time to leave.

Its loyalties were more Florentine than Sienese, and at Grand Duke Ferdinand I's death in 1609 he left it as a legacy to his wife Christina of Lorraine, who ruled the town for thirty years like a little principality, issuing her own coins as 'Cristina Lotharinga Magna Ducissa Etruriae Domina Montis Politiani'. Nobody seems to know who the original Politianus was who gave a name to the mountain, but it was a sobriquet eagerly adopted by that most attractive of renaissance humanists Angelo Ambrogini, known to us for ever as Poliziano.

Poliziano's short life (he was born in 1454 and died in 1494) was devoted to an insatiable desire for reading and learning. Loyal to the Medici for the sake of his father, murdered in their service, he became the friend of Lorenzo and tutor to his son. As a lecturer and commentator on Greek authors he was unrivalled and as a translator he was indefatigable. For the court of Mantua, during a temporary exile, he took two days to

This well, at Montepulciano, crowned with the Medici arms, was built in 1520.

compose his *Orfeo*, a musical drama foreshadowing the invention of opera a century later, and one of the great literary works of the age. As for his poetry, its freshness and vivacity are authentically Tuscan, free from the dragging weight of scholarship or the gravity Poliziano must have needed to assume as secretary and propagandist at the Medici court.

His house is practically the first notable thing beyond the Porta delle Farine as you enter the town from the Chianciano road, leaving behind a phenomenal panorama across eastern hills and valleys. Up Via Vannuzzi beyond this is the Teatro Poliziano, charmingly restored for the festivals. In white and gold with touches of Pompeian red, its auditorium, with a ceiling of assembled poets (including Shakespeare and Goldoni), is a typical horseshoe of boxes on the traditional model for Italian theatres from Turin to Palermo, so thrilling to those who love the kind of lyric opera they were built to contain.

To the left, on the other hand, past the usual Medici fortress and down a lime-shaded avenue, is the church of Santa Maria dei Servi, where a gothic façade conceals a baroque interior of restrained sophistication by the northern architect Andrea dal Pozzo (1642–1709), whose work can be seen elsewhere in Montepulciano. Striking uphill from here I like to walk slowly and euphorically along the town's narrow spine, with something to delight the eye at every turn.

Almost parallel with the theatre stands the cathedral, with its eternally unfinished brick front. The simple, well-lit renaissance building of 1592–1630 is by Ippolito Scalza and contains two of Montepulciano's treasures, the enormous polyptych of the *Assumption* by Taddeo di Bartolo (1363–1422) over the high altar, and whatever remains of the tomb of Bartolomeo Aragazzi, the work of Michelozzo. Taddeo, who worked mostly in Siena between 1380 and 1420, is one of those painters about whom we know so little that they recall Oscar Wilde's notorious 'I have

203

nothing to declare but my genius'. This genius was truly lavished on a massive but never pompous composition, where the Madonna is borne heavenwards above a group of weeping apostles. As for Michelozzo's elegant sepulchre, begun in 1427, this was dismantled during the seventeenth century, and surviving fragments are scattered around the church. The finely-modelled statue is placed beside the west door and decorative pieces line the nave: could some attempt not be made to reassemble them?

The front of the *duomo* gives on to an exceptionally dignified Piazza Grande, one of the best illustrations I know of what open spaces in an Italian city really mean. Grand it may be, but its grandeur is as vivid, lively and good-looking as the people moving across it. Here is the medieval Palazzo Comunale, with its thrusting battlemented tower, from whose top you can see the whole of southern Tuscany and Umbria as far as Assisi. Opposite is the learned yet unstuffy classicism of Antonio da Sangallo's Palazzo Contucci of 1519, and next to this are the beautiful *loggic* of Palazzo Tarugi by the Modenese architect Jacopo Barozzi (1507–73), known as Vignola from his Apennine birthplace. And as if these were not enough blessings upon this blessed little city, there is Palazzo Neri Orselli, best Sienese brick-built gothic, down Via Ricci. Here the Museo Civico mingles Byzantine illuminated manuscripts, a *Madonna and Child* by Sodoma and a *Magdalen* by the talented late sixteenth-century Pisan artist Lodovico Cigoli.

Via Ricci becomes Via Mazzini and palace succeeds to palace with all the impact-making contrast of one of Serlio's ideal stage sets. The baroque church of Santa Lucia holds a damaged Signorelli *Madonna*, and the

The sixteenth-century Palazzo Tarugi at Montepulciano is attributed to the Modenese architect Iacopo Vignola.

Above A delicately modelled lunette by Michelozzo above the main doorway of Sant'Agostino, Montepulciano.

Right The Madonna di San Biagio, outside Montepulciano, is the masterpiece of Antonio da Sangallo.

façade of Sant' Agostino, where you rejoin the main drag of the Via Roma, is Michelozzo in nostalgic Florentine gothic mood, adorning the lunette above the garlanded portal with a *Virgin and Child* and attendant saints. Beyond this, at the town's north gate, stands Andrea dal Pozzo's miniature gem of an oval baroque chapel to St Bernard.

The most ravishing surprise of all is reserved for those leaving Montepulciano by the Pienza road. Up an alley of cypresses stands the church of the Madonna di San Biagio, begun in 1518 by Antonio da Sangallo. In colour alone, a deeply ripened yellow, it is handsome enough, but the design, with its admiring reference to Bramante, constitutes one of the purest architectural interpretations of the classical style, and its influence can be felt echoing across Europe. The relationships of line and contour here are as perfect as the formal balance between sober pedimented façades and the curve of the dome. Only one of its twin *campanili* was ever completed, but this paradoxically lends a more effective accent to the ensemble.

Join the main road northwards, which crosses a markedly southern-looking countryside towards Torrita di Siena. Here there are still a few fragments of the towers suggested by its name, and at least two good pictures in the *pieve*, a *Nativity* by Bartolo di Fredi (1330–1410) and a *Madonna and Child* by Benvenuto di Giovanni, who painted mostly in Siena during the second half of the fifteenth century. There are even better works by Benvenuto at Sinalunga, along the edge of the steep valley, but if lunchtime arrives and you are still on the road it is worth halting at the Fattoria dell' Amorosa, a typical farm-cum-village of the region, which includes a fine restaurant in the old stables.

A gothic doorway to the parish church of Monticchiello, west of Montepulciano.

Sinalunga started life as Asinalunga – 'the long gulf' – a defensive outpost of the Sienese *contado*, only passing to Florentine control after the defeat in 1363 of the appalling Company of the Hat, a band of bullying soldiers-of-fortune terrorizing the area. Bellicose associations clung to the place during later centuries: in 1867 the government of newly united Italy rounded up Garibaldi himself here and had him deported to the island of Caprera before he could march on Rome, still in Papal hands. But the old lion finally got away, only to be defeated by the French at Mentana. The Sinalunga arrest was thoroughly good-mannered, since the officers involved insisted that Garibaldi finished his bath before they marched him away.

Apart from a Sodoma *Madonna* in the sixteenth-century Collegiata, most of the really good pictures are in the small Franciscan church of San Bernardino, beside its convent at the top of a cypress avenue. On the right-hand wall of the choir hangs Benvenuto's tender but never mawkish *Annunciation* and opposite is a *Virgin and Saints* by Sano di Pietro. I have a special affection for Sano, routinely pooh-poohed by art historians partly for his sheer fecundity; his compositions radiate a childlike certainty and cheerfulness which makes him infinitely more engaging than some of his loftier Sienese contemporaries.

Keeping due north cross the valley to Lucignano, capping the green hill with its concentric rings of houses around a grandiose, lantern-domed Collegiata of 1594 with a lavishly baroque high altar by Andrea dal Pozzo. Behind this is the Museo Civico, sheltering some unexpectedly fine works which, taken together, form a microcosm of Sienese art, with its stress on sinuous forms, delicate textures and the resistless impact of decoration. The town itself, without the usual dribble of suburban *bijou* residences, retains the spirit of its medieval foundation, though the unfinished Medici fortress on a nearby hilltop adds an incongruously mournful note to the landscape.

209

Finally to one of my favourite spots in Tuscany, potently expressive of what the small Italian hill town really means in terms of richly layered human experience mirrored in the synthesis of its building materials and architectural styles. Monte San Savino looks oddly defenceless on its little spur above the lush Val di Chiana, but it was bitterly fought over by Guelph and Ghibelline and in 1325 Bishop Tarlati of Arezzo ordered its wholesale destruction. Rebuilt, it survived famine, plague and siege, passing from one overlord to another only to be scooped up by the Grand Duke in 1747.

The town's inordinate civic pride is mirrored in a plethora of *targhe*, those marble slabs with sonorous inscriptions in a form of extra-pompous Italian used solely in this context, commemorating local boys made good. Such indeed were Giuseppe Sanarelli, discoverer of the yellow fever bacillus, the great Etruscan archaeologist Gamurrini, and the Jewish poet Salomone Fiorentino. During his time, in 1799, the 'Viva Maria' riots broke out in Arezzo and the resulting wave of pious anti-semitism, so uncharacteristic of Italy, spread to Monte San Savino. On 7 May the little Jewish community in Via del Ghetto was rounded up and massacred in the central piazza, but though the synagogue and rabbi's house can still be seen, the few Jews who managed to escape never came back.

Most illustrious among *savinesi* was the sculptor Andrea Contucci. Known as Sansovino (1460–1529), he was among the most versatile of those influenced by the young Michelangelo (the older artist had his eye on the block of marble which ultimately became Michelangelo's *David*). We can see his work at its best in the church of Santa Chiara, built in 1652, close to the northern Porta Fiorentina and beautiful in the disparity of its treasures flung together in the small, dark interior like a pirate's spoils. Sansovino's altarpiece of SS Laurence, Roch and Sebastian, in its border of lush fruit and flower swags, was his earliest major work, brought here from the demolished church of Sant'Agata. Even lovelier is the glazed terracotta tabernacle on the left of the high altar, with the figures of SS Lucy and Romualdo in niches beside the kneeling Agatha and Augustine adoring the Madonna and Child, a joint composition by Sansovino and Andrea della Robbia, in which the modelling of the draperies is so exquisitely airy that you can almost hear them rustling. Another quartet of saints on two painted panels form part of a dismembered triptych by Guidoccio Cozzarelli (1450–1516), their effectiveness heightened by a palette carefully limited to black, gold and red.

Opposite the church, in the Piazza Gamurrini (originally called Jalta, 'Area Alta', after the earliest settlement), the *savinesi* sought to honour their feudal governor Mattias de' Medici with the obelisk in the centre. When they had raised it, the prudent prince ordered that 'seeing that the community of the Principality is more and more encumbered with debts, in particular because of the monument . . . no further expenditures be made'.

The place was grand enough as it was. Down the main Corso stands the overwhelmingly grand Palazzo di Monte, built by Cardinal Antonio di Monte, member of one of the town's first families, in 1515, when Antonio da Sangallo was given the commission. The synthesis between rusticated lower storey and upper floor with pedimented windows and Ionic pillars is admirably conceived, as is the colonnaded courtyard. At the back, completed by Nanni di Baccio Bigio under Antonio's nephew Giovanni Maria, who became Pope Julius III in 1550, the remains of a formal garden spread southwards to the rampart wall.

Fantasy transforms a helmeted Italian soldier of the Great War into a winged legionary at Monte San Savino.

211

On the other side of the street from the palace is Sansovino's Corinthian Loggia dei Mercanti of 1518–20, which once sheltered a market for silk cocoons and a granary but which is now the favoured place for the town's youth to congregate with their *motorini* and eat ices. Further down past the restored baroque *pieve*, with its arcaded west end which provides the keynote for the town's churches, is Sant'Agostino, where this feature is enhanced by the presence of two frescoed walls by Giovanni d'Agnolo di Balduccio (1370–1452). Under the left-hand arch is a busy *Adoration of the Magi*: contrast this with a sober *Presentation in the Temple* in the lunette, with its companion *Crucifixion*. Over the high altar Vasari lays on the spectacular in a colourful *Assumption*, flanked by works by his versatile pupil Orazio Porta.

With any luck there will be an exhibition in the Cassero, the town's old citadel, to one side of Piazza Gamurrini. Even if what is being shown (generally ceramics) is dull, you can get marvellous glimpses across the countryside towards Castiglion Fiorentino or Arezzo, to which you can now return via the north gate. The road to Arezzo is relentlessly straight and fearsomely dull, as I should know, for I once walked the fourteen odd miles of it one August morning when the operators of the one-track *trenino* going all the way down to Chiusi had decided that this was the day on which they were to dig up the line.

But *forza, ragazzi!*, for here the fennel-stuffed chicken and tagliolini of Arezzo await us, with a bottle of what Doctor Redi calls '*la manna di Montepulciano*'. We have earned it, after all.

A solitary olive tree grows to look like a cypress, in a field near Monte San Savino.

Index

215